Advanced Pathfinder **4**
Managing coursework

Other titles in the series

Tests and targets (APF3)
Ted Neather

Developing learning strategies (APF2)
Barry Jones

Advancing oral skills (APF1)
Anneli McLachlan

Centre for Information
on Language Teaching and Research

The Centre for Information on Language Teaching and
Research provides a complete range of services for
language professionals in every stage and sector of
education, and in business, in support of its brief to
promote Britain's foreign language capability.

CILT is a registered charity, supported by Central
Government grants. CILT is based in Covent Garden,
London, and its services are delivered through a
national collaborative network of regional Comenius
Centres in England, CILT Cymru, Northern Ireland
CILT and Scottish CILT.

advan̲ced
Pathfinder
4

Managing coursework

COLIN CHRISTIE

Centre for Information
on Language Teaching and Research

The views expressed in this publication are the author's and do not necessarily represent those of CILT.

Acknowledgements

The author and publisher would like to thank copyright holders for permission granted to reproduce copyright material, as detailed next to the relevant excerpts.

In some cases it has not been possible to trace copyright holders of material reproduced in this book. The publisher will be pleased to make the appropriate arrangement with any copyright holder whom it has not been possible to contact at the earliest opportunity.

First published 2002 by the Centre for Information on Language Teaching and Research (CILT), 20 Bedfordbury, London, WC2N 4LB

ISBN 1 902031 98 9

A catalogue record for this book is available from the British Library

Printed in Great Britain by Copyprint UK Ltd

CILT Publications are available from: **Central Books**, 99 Wallis Rd, London E9 5LN. Tel: 0845 458 9910. Fax: 0845 458 9912. Book trade representation (UK and Ireland): **Broadcast Book Services**, Charter House, 27a London Road, Croydon CR0 2RE. Tel: 020 8681 8949. Fax: 020 8688 0615.

> **P** All pages marked with this symbol are photocopiable for use with your students.

Acknowledgements

I would like to thank Heinemann Educational for permission to reproduce their materials in this book. I would also like to thank Aimée-Shirin Daruwala, Michael Evans, Linda Fisher, Barry Jones, John Kinnear for providing the Spanish material and writing the case study on film, Deborah Manning, Anneli McLachlan, Ursula Mulla, Alesha Neeamuth, Emma Rees, Béatrix Roudet, Hiltrud Starke, Kerin White and Anke Wilkens for their invaluable input. I would also like to thank the A level students of Newham Sixth Form College and Elliott School for their commitment and enthusiasm which have made this book possible.

Introduction

This book aims to set out the requirements of A level coursework and offer effective approaches to the planning, organising and managing of students' learning and work.

Coursework at A2 examines three of the four assessment objectives laid down in the subject criteria for Modern Foreign Languages (MFL):

AO2: understand and respond, in (speech and) writing, to written language.

AO3: show knowledge of and apply accurately the grammar and syntax prescribed in the specification.

AO4: demonstrate knowledge and understanding of aspects of the chosen society.

This book begins by examining the advantages of coursework for the student and the impact it has on the teacher's planning and teaching. Sometimes teachers may be reluctant to adopt the coursework option because of the increased demands it makes upon the teacher. We shall therefore look at strategies for coping with the process at each stage so that common problems are anticipated. It is, however, significant that the coursework option is now favoured by the majority of centres over the terminal examination. In the case of OCR, for example, approximately 70% of candidates now take the coursework option.

Planning for coursework is essential from the beginning of the A2 year, or the end of the AS year if possible. It tends to be much less successful if it is an add-on or if students are left to their own devices to produce what they can.

The teacher will need to ask a series of questions which we shall consider in detail:

- Which topics?
- When?
- What sort of writing?
- How can I monitor what the students are doing?
- How do I know which resources to use?
- How can I ensure students will produce work of an acceptable standard?

In turn, students will be faced with a number of decisions and it is to our advantage if we can help them to make the right choices before they encounter problems. It is far more time-consuming to undo the result of a student's poor choices than it is to lead him or her into making the right choice from the outset. We should guide students through the coursework maze but at the same allow them to make key decisions for themselves.

The student will be asking:

- Which aspect of a topic should I consider?
- What should my title be?
- How can I get the necessary information?
- How do I know my language will be up to scratch?
- When and where do I start?

As daunting as some of these questions may seem, this book will show that with the necessary preparation the student can have the confidence to deal with them successfully one by one.

Apart from managing the overall process of coursework, we need to ensure that we are equipping students with the skills they will need to undertake it. Many of these are applicable to other aspects of the course or will have been displayed at AS level, such as research skills. Students will need to be able to:

- identify appropriate sources from a whole range;
- extract relevant facts, statistics and quotations;
- extract appropriate topic-related lexis and useful structures;
- organise material coherently and incorporate research;
- understand different written genres;
- decide upon a focused title for their coursework;
- plan and structure written work carefully;
- provide opinions and sequence them logically;
- use language of quality and demonstrate a range of lexis and structures;
- manage their time well;
- review and evaluate their work.

Many of these skills will have been developed at AS level and will simply need building upon. Others, such as structured writing, may need more practice.

These are all skills we can teach. Preparation of students in this way will result in more effective pieces of coursework.

Managing coursework gives practical advice and ideas for coping with coursework for higher level examinations and the new style A2 examination, from beginning to end. The book is organised into chapters dealing with coursework rationale, organisation, preparation, research and study skills, the student's planning and finally the writing and reviewing. Case studies are provided at the end of the book, suggesting approaches in three languages and giving ideas on how to approach three different types of coursework.

The suggested approaches and checklists on pages marked **P** are photocopiable for classroom use.

1

Why do coursework?

Coursework is a great motivator for students. So often in language work, the student has simply to learn specified vocabulary, or come to grips with prescribed grammatical structures and has little scope for independent study or self-expression. Coursework is a real opportunity to explore an area in depth and give a piece of work a personal slant.

Reasons students give for enjoying coursework:

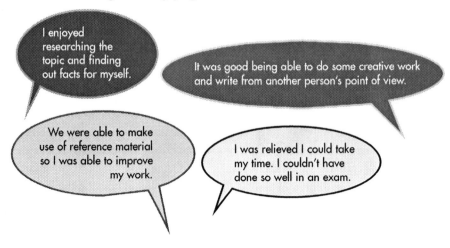

I enjoyed researching the topic and finding out facts for myself.

It was good being able to do some creative work and write from another person's point of view.

We were able to make use of reference material so I was able to improve my work.

I was relieved I could take my time. I couldn't have done so well in an exam.

Students at GCSE often point out that the content of the syllabus does not allow them to explore their own interests and study any area in detail. While AS and A level do address this problem, there is rarely time to explore aspects of a topic in any depth, especially during the AS year. Coursework can satisfy students' desire to learn more about the target language country and write in a personal way. They are also often pleased that it means they do not have to write extensively under examination conditions as the coursework element replaces the 'Prescribed Topics and Texts' paper.

Here is a summary of the advantages of coursework:

- ✔ Students gain research skills and read extensively.
- ✔ There is the chance to pursue personal interests and to show initiative.
- ✔ A variety of sources can be used, broadening students' involvement with the target-language (TL) culture.
- ✔ Independent, in-depth study is promoted and students can work at their own pace.
- ✔ Students develop skills of planning, analysis and synthesis.
- ✔ There is the opportunity for creativity both in terms of media used and approach taken.
- ✔ Visits abroad and penfriend communications can be given a focus.
- ✔ No terminal examination for this module.
- ✔ An opportunity to develop and claim key skills.

Coursework requirements

Requirements for coursework vary between the boards. The following table highlights what is required by each board:

Board	Length	Assessment	Deadline
AQA	2 pieces, each 700 words	15%	mid-May
Edexcel	Piece 1: 450–500 words Piece 2: 900–1000 words	5% 10%	1st May
OCR	Total: 1200–1400 words EITHER one piece OR two pieces x 600–700 words	15 %	mid-May

As well as being written independently by the student, coursework needs to include the following for it to meet the examination board's requirements and represent a valid body of study:

- ▪ Extensive reading in the target language.
- ▪ Dealing with the target-language country/culture.
- ▪ The involvement of individual research and addressing of personal interests.

More detailed requirements are that:

- each piece of coursework should cover a very distinct and separate area of study. This should not overlap with the prepared oral topic either;
- students in one teaching group do not all submit work with the same title.

Beyond simply meeting the requirements, teachers will want to ensure their students' coursework gains the highest possible marks. We shall see that several factors such as the choice of title, availability of resources and the planning process, make for a **good** piece of coursework.

Coursework counts for 15% of the final examination marks.

Assessment criteria

It is an almost automatic response to judge the quality of a piece of written work by the quality of the language. Poor spelling and grammar immediately create a bad impression and suggest the work has not been carefully planned and produced. We must, however, bear in mind the mark allocations given to language and content before we make this sort of judgement. Marks for each piece of coursework are not distributed evenly between language and content but are allocated using the following assessment criteria:

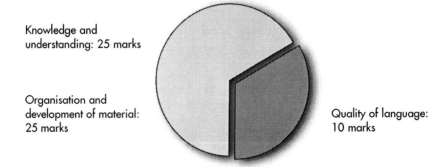

Knowledge and understanding: 25 marks

Organisation and development of material: 25 marks

Quality of language: 10 marks

(Edexcel)

AQA and OCR proportions are given in Appendix 1 on p65.

As we can see from the chart above, while quality of language might create a good/bad impression of a student's work, in terms of assessment, content and structure are weighted more heavily. In the case of Edexcel here, content is weighted over language by 5:1. It is, therefore, crucial that we always look beyond the language to the content when advising students and assessing work.

Let us look more closely at what examiners are looking for. In the Edexcel syllabus, for example, the criteria are usefully broken down as follows:

Knowledge and understanding

- knowledge and understanding of the topic
- grasp of the implications and scope of the topic
- relevance, clarity of thought and expression, ability to analyse
- ability to use evidence and source material
- independent judgement/originality
- imaginative personal response to the source material, where appropriate

Organisation and development of material

- planning, organisation and control of material
- logical and effective sequencing of material
- ability to develop argument and ideas

Quality of language

- ability to communicate intelligibly
- accuracy
- variety of structures
- appropriateness of language
- lexical range
- fluency

This looks like a plethora of different marking criteria but, in fact, many of the areas are inter-related. As with all skills, it is important to share these criteria with students from the outset. That way they can plan and organise their work in order to gain the highest marks possible. The checklist on p9 can be copied and handed to students in the initial stages of planning their coursework to help them understand what examiners are looking for.

We shall now consider the top level descriptor in each category to help us focus on what teachers need to encourage students to demonstrate in their coursework.

	Knowledge and understanding
24-25	Exceptional k/u. Fully relevant and clear-sighted. Shows excellent insight into the theme(s), a very high degree of independent judgement, and wholly convincing use of evidence and source material **or** outstanding response to the stimulus material and fully convincing use of it in creative writing.
	Organisation and development of material
24-25	Exceptional o/d. A high degree of logic and coherence throughout. Very skilful handling of often complex material.
	Quality of language
9-10	Excellent communication. Language almost always fluent, varied and appropriate. Wide range of lexis and structures. High level of accuracy.

Source: Edexcel

Student task: Look at the mark grid and, in pairs, pick out ten key words which highlight what an excellent piece of coursework should look like. You can alter words and phrases if you think this makes your answer clearer. Compare your answer with the list below.

Here is a suggested list of answers:

- relevant
- clear
- own opinions
- convincing
- logical

- different sections fit together well
- easily understood and easy to read
- wide range of vocabulary
- different structures used
- accurate.

We shall explore at greater length how to help students meet these criteria but for the present the checklist gives a useful overview. The list on the following page helps to share this overview with students. It is not intended to help them choose a topic or title – this advice can be found in other parts of this book. It does, however, give them an idea of what will gain them good marks and shows them what they are aiming for once they start writing. It is, in other words, the examination criteria in student-friendly language.

What is the examiner looking for in a good piece of coursework?

Keep this list safe and refer to it as you proceed with your planning and writing.

To gain the best marks, I will need to make sure my coursework ... ✔

- answers the question and does not discuss areas that do not relate to the question . . . . ☐
- explains which part of the question I am answering as I go along . . . ☐
- gives my **own** reactions and opinions, not just those I have read . . . ☐
- refers to a number of target-language sources, not just one . . . . ☐
- includes facts and statistics gained from what I have read/seen/ heard . . . . ☐
- uses (and acknowledges) quotations from my sources . . . . ☐

  (For a piece of creative writing:
- is written in the right style: of a character/of a newspaper, etc) . . . . . ☐
- deals with each point in a logical order, one at a time. . . . . ☐
- links one section to the next, using sub-headings where necessary. . . ☐
- uses a good number of phrases I have adapted and know to be correct. . . . . ☐
- does not use sentences I have translated straight from English and have not checked. . . . . ☐
- does not use sentences that are too long. ☐
- uses topic-related vocabulary. . . . . ☐
- uses a variety of vocabulary. . . . . ☐
- uses different grammatical structures. . . . . ☐
- is re-read a couple of days after writing and checked for accuracy. . . ☐

key points

- Coursework is a motivating option for students.
- Familiarise yourself with the examination board's requirements and assessment criteria.
- Share the above with your students from the outset and analyse what makes a good piece of coursework.
- Focus on content as this attracts the majority of marks (but not to the exclusion of accurate and varied language).

Organising coursework

The key to a good piece of coursework is good organisation, both on the part of the teacher and the student. Coursework is not intended to be entirely taught, but rather to be a student's individual response, nor should it be viewed as a totally separate element of the course. Difficulties can arise if the student is given free rein to choose his or her own topic, totally independently of the teacher and the course. This results in extra work, both for the teacher (researching a possibly unfamiliar topic and identifying source material) and for the student (having to research and organise work from scratch, with no foundation on which to build).

One good model for coursework is for it to flow from a general topic area already covered in class which is then extended and developed as in the following model.

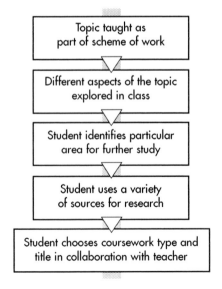

Here is an example of how this might work in practice:

French				
General topic	Société			
Specific area within that topic	Immigration		Education	
Specific aspect within that area	Intégration	Racisme	Réformes	Violence
Essay 1	Le rôle d'une radio Associative, Radio Soleil, dans l'intégration des Africains du Nord.	Analyse du comportement raciste dans un incident spécifique	L'effet des réformes récentes sur le statut des professeurs des collèges.	A quoi peut-on attribuer la violence au lycée de...?
Essay 2	La société française de nos jours est-elle une société pluriculturelle?	Le Front National a-t-il eu un effet durable sur la vie en France?	Les réformes récentes ont-elles amélioré l'éducation en France?	Le problème de la violence dans les écoles en France peut-il être résolu?

Source: Edexcel

It can be seen, then, that coursework requires planning on a departmental basis and incorporating into a scheme of work if it is to be delivered successfully. Some topics lend themselves to coursework more easily than others.

Here is a checklist for an effective coursework topic:

- ☑ relates to the TL country;
- ☑ engages students' interests, i.e. it is not too abstract;
- ☑ contains a number of sub-topics to allow different interpretations;
- ☑ invites a personal response;
- ☑ allows students to progress beyond the descriptive and invites detailed analysis;
- ☑ has scope for creative writing;
- ☑ teacher has a good knowledge of the topic;
- ☑ teacher has access to a variety of resources, preferably using different media.

A student version of this checklist is available on p66 in Appendix 2.

Different coursework styles

There are different types of coursework study possible as long as they meet the criteria above.

These types are:

- Study of a topic or issue in the TL culture: 'Drugs', 'Immigration', etc.
- Study of a work of literature or the comparison of two or more works.
- Study of one or more film(s).

It is worth emphasising that any topic studied must not be context-free. It is not permissible, for example, for students to write on the threats to the environment in the 21st century. They must always refer to the context of the TL country or culture. They might, therefore, discuss issues around nuclear power demonstrations in Germany or undertake a study of recycling initiatives in France.

The last point on our earlier checklist above, concerning resources, is particularly relevant. Teachers and students can identify some superb topic titles but if the department has few up-to-date resources relating to them, then not only will there be a lack of information but the topics will become dry and tedious.

Do you have enough supporting material to teach a film or book? Are there enough resources available on a given topic?

You are not, of course, restricted to one type of study or another. It is possible to combine different types of coursework study, for example, the comparison of a book and the film of the book, or a topic such as juvenile delinquency, with examples taken from fictional literature.

Planning time

While the independence of the student should be encouraged, it is also important to set clear guidelines for time management. A student will almost certainly find the organisation and planning of coursework alone a daunting task. Overwhelmed by the enormity of the task he or she may well not get started until it is too late and end up producing work that is rushed and sub-standard. To avoid this happening, students can be issued with A3 size planners indicating certain deadlines. If they are to produce two pieces of work, the planner may include the following deadlines:

Draft plan for Piece 1 Date:		Draft plan for Piece 2 Date:
Plan for Piece 1 Date:		Plan for Piece 2 Date:
Draft of Piece 1 Date:		Draft of Piece 2 Date:
Final draft of Piece 1 Date:		Final draft of Piece 2 Date:
Bibliography for Piece 1 Date:		Bibliography for Piece 2 Date:
Completed plan, coursework and bibliography: *mid-January*		Completed plan, coursework and bibliography: *mid-April*

While, in accordance with the board's regulations, the draft piece of coursework may not be marked, it is helpful for the teacher to see that the student is working according to schedule.

Depending on the department, you may well wish to add a deadline for 'List of resources to be used' and/or 'Completed research notes'. This helps to break down an onerous task into smaller, more manageable sections. It also allows the teacher to monitor that work is being done towards the final piece and not to be fooled by a promise that 'work is in progress'!

Once again, this should be a department-wide policy. It can be very confusing for a double linguist if this sort of planning is implemented in one language but not another and might lead to his or her taking the work less seriously.

In terms of when the pieces should be submitted in the context of the course as a whole, the following suggestion may be helpful:

Piece 1 completed by mid-January	Piece 2 completed by mid-April

These deadlines will vary from establishment to establishment but need to take into account time for marking and feeding back on piece 1 and for marking and sending off the work for piece 2.

The role of the teacher

The continuum below illustrates the varying degree of help which could be offered to a student:

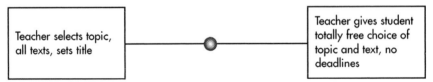

Teacher selects topic, all texts, sets title

Teacher gives student totally free choice of topic and text, no deadlines

It should be clear that neither end of the spectrum represents good practice. It is important to maintain a balance. One should give as much guidance as possible while respecting the board's regulations and the student's independence.

Here is a suggested list of do's and don't's for the teacher. We shall look at each area in more depth in the coming chapters.

DO	DON'T
☑ Teach a topic in general terms.	☒ Allow a student to choose an unsuitable topic (however much it may interest him or her!) or one which has not had at least some teaching input.
☑ Provide a list of resources and a selection from which to choose.	
☑ Set clear deadlines.	
☑ Discuss the choice of topic and title with the student.	☒ Allow a student to use English resources.
☑ Discuss the full draft plan in detail with the student.	☒ Forget to monitor the student's work so that two days before the final deadline no work has been done!
☑ Provide feedback after the first piece of coursework.	☒ Give feedback once the final plan has been agreed (exam board regulations).

key points

- Plan teaching topics carefully, ensuring there is the scope for a good piece of coursework.
- Ensure sufficient and appropriate resources are available for any given topic.
- Guide the student carefully in the choice of topic.
- Give students clear, achievable deadlines, breaking down the task as much as possible.

3

Preparing for coursework

It has already been mentioned that only certain topics are suitable for coursework and that they should ideally be introduced in class. It is important, however, not to cover in too much depth an area which will form a part of a student's coursework. In particular, the teacher should not ask students to write on exactly the same issues which they might later wish to choose for coursework. Not only does this contravene the examination boards' rules but it also deprives the student of the opportunity to do some research and discover new ideas and facts for him or herself.

We shall look at the three types of coursework and offer suggestions as to how one may go about teaching an area with coursework in mind. Obviously, much of what is suggested may form part of our everyday teaching, whether or not we choose to give students the opportunity to do coursework. Nevertheless, it is hoped that the approaches given below will enable teacher and student to cope with coursework in the most effective way while still remaining within exam board rules.

Choosing the topic or issue

When choosing to teach a topic which will lead to coursework, it is wise (as pointed out in Chapter 2) to pick a general area which can be broken down into further sub-sections for coursework purposes.

Students of mine have produced coursework on the topic of TV, for example, taught as a sub-section of the topic 'media'. The topic of 'media' is broad enough to allow them to choose an area of interest to them and interpret it in an individual way.

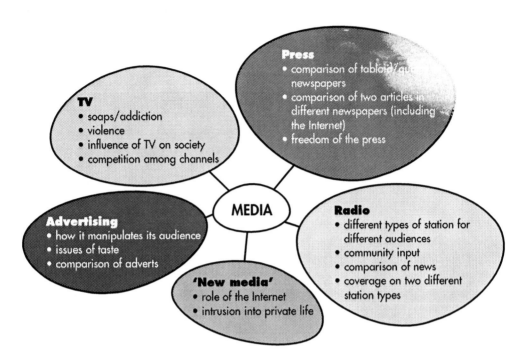

The sub-division of a topic not only allows students to explore different areas, in line with coursework guidelines, but also offers a variety of response: analysing texts, discussing generally or making detailed comparisons. Some students find it easier to compare specific texts, e.g. newspaper articles, while others are better at giving a general overview.

It is at the discretion of the teacher how the topic is approached and how much of it is taught directly. Nevertheless, the following suggested approach to the topic of 'media' is a useful guide.

Approaching a coursework topic: Media

1. Give a general overview of different types of media, conduct a survey of students' viewing/reading/listening habits and of the use of media by people living in the TL country; work on specialist vocabulary.

A survey like this one could be used to elicit an initial personal response to the topic:

8.1 Warum sehen Sie fern?

8 Die Medien

Zu zweit arbeiten! Tragen Sie die eigenen Motivationen auf Formular A ein. Überlegen Sie, wie ihr/e Partner/in das Formular ausgefüllt hat und versuchen Sie, seine/ihre Antworten auf Formular B vorherzusagen. Vergleichen Sie dann die Bewertungen. Wer kennt die Fernsehmotive des/der anderen besser?

Formular A

Überprüfen Sie Ihre Fernsehmotive!

Welche der zehn Aussagen trifft wie oft auf Sie zu?

1 oft   2 manchmal   3 selten   4 nie

Ich sehe fern, …	1	2	3	4
1 Weil es so interessant und spannend ist.	☐	☐	☐	☐
2 Weil die Clique sehr viel über TV-Sendungen redet.	☐	☐	☐	☐
3 Weil ich nichts Besseres zu tun habe.	☐	☐	☐	☐
4 Weil ich der Realität entrinnen möchte.	☐	☐	☐	☐
5 Weil ich etwas über Sachen wissen möchte, von denen ich sonst nichts höre.	☐	☐	☐	☐
6 Weil ich sehen will, was in der Welt so alles los ist.	☐	☐	☐	☐
7 Weil wir dann in der Familie beisammen sind.	☐	☐	☐	☐
8 Weil ich dabei lerne, wie sich andere verhalten.	☐	☐	☐	☐
9 Weil die Glotze schon eingeschaltet ist.	☐	☐	☐	☐
10 Weil ich mich entspannen will.	☐	☐	☐	☐

Formular B

Überprüfen Sie Ihre Fernsehmotive!

Welche der zehn Aussagen trifft wie oft auf Sie zu?

1 oft   2 manchmal   3 selten   4 nie

Ich sehe fern, …	1	2	3	4
1 Weil es so interessant und spannend ist.	☐	☐	☐	☐
2 Weil die Clique sehr viel über TV-Sendungen redet.	☐	☐	☐	☐
3 Weil ich nichts Besseres zu tun habe.	☐	☐	☐	☐
4 Weil ich der Realität entrinnen möchte.	☐	☐	☐	☐
5 Weil ich etwas über Sachen wissen möchte, von denen ich sonst nichts höre.	☐	☐	☐	☐
6 Weil ich sehen will, was in der Welt so alles los ist.	☐	☐	☐	☐
7 Weil wir dann in der Familie beisammen sind.	☐	☐	☐	☐
8 Weil ich dabei lerne, wie sich andere verhalten.	☐	☐	☐	☐
9 Weil die Glotze schon eingeschaltet ist.	☐	☐	☐	☐
10 Weil ich mich entspannen will.	☐	☐	☐	☐

Source: Brennpunkt neue Ausgabe © Sandry, Somerville, Morris & Aberdeen (Nelson, 2000)

Giving students some views for them to agree/disagree with starts focusing the mind on the issues involved and also starts them working with the relevant vocabulary. French and Spanish versions of the survey overleaf are provided in Appendices 3 and 5, pp67 and 76.

GEWALT IM FERNSEHEN

Umfrage: beantworten Sie 'Ja' oder 'Nein':

	Ja	Nein
1. Das Fernsehen ist eine Droge.	○	○
2. Es gibt zu viel Gewalt im Fernsehen.	○	○
3. Kinder sollten nie vor dem Fernseher allein gelassen werden.	○	○
4. Gewalttätige Filme machen manche Leute auch gewalttätig.	○	○
5. Kinder können nicht zwischen Bild und Wirklichkeit unterscheiden.	○	○
6. Die Eltern sind daran schuld, dass ihre Kinder zu viel fernsehen.	○	○
7. Viele Eltern benutzen den Fernseher als Babysitter.	○	○
8. Die Zuschauer sollten vor Gewalt gewarnt werden.	○	○
9. Gewalt im Fernsehen ist manchmal nötig und sogar hilfreich.	○	○
10. Bei Filmen sollte es keine Zensur geben.	○	○

2. Teach lessons focusing on each of the sub-sections: TV, Press, Advertising, New Media. These can begin by surveying the landscape and move towards the learning of specialist vocabulary and the highlighting of specific issues in the TL country.

At every stage, students should be looking at texts, watching videos, listening to extracts and undertaking exercises with a view to picking out specialist vocabulary and learning how to use it as it stands and/or to rephrase it. Here is an example of exercises which help students develop specialist vocabulary on the topic of the environment in an active way, as opposed to simply presenting them with a pre-prepared list to learn.

1 a Umweltprobleme. Finden Sie das passende Wortende zu jedem Wortanfang. Suchen Sie dabei die richtige Bedeutung aus.

1	Treibhaus-	a	-gesellschaft
2	Ozon-	b	-kraft
3	Luft-	c	-belästigung
4	Verkehrs-	d	-verschmutzung
5	Gefahren der Atom-	e	-lawine
6	Wald-	f	-pest
7	Energie-	g	-loch
8	Lärm-	h	-sterben
9	Wegwerf-	i	-verschwendung
10	Algen-	j	-effekt

Bedeutungen:

A Wenn man zu viel Strom verbraucht.
B Wenn die Atmosphäre unrein ist.
C Wenn Bäume abgeholzt bzw. getötet werden.
D Wenn die Erde verheizt wird.
E Wenn es zu laut wird.
F Wenn die See grün wird.
G Die große Zunahme an Autos.
H Durch FCKWs verursachter Schaden.
I Wenn die Öffentlichkeit wenig recycelt.
J Probleme der Kernkraft.

b Können Sie vereinfachte Definitionen von „Ozonloch" und „Treibhauseffekt" für Kinder schreiben, in denen Sie alle Fachausdrücke vermeiden?

c Ordnen Sie die Liste nach Wichtigkeit (Nummer 1 = größte Gefahr).

d Klassendiskussion: Vergleichen Sie Ihre Ergebnisse und besprechen Sie die sinnvollste Reihenfolge. Seien Sie bereit, einen Kompromiss zu schließen!

- Wenn Sie einverstanden sind, sagen Sie:
  Ich bin ganz Ihrer Meinung.
  Da gebe ich Ihnen Recht.
  Das stimmt.
  Ich bin völlig einverstanden.
  Das finde ich auch.

- Wenn Sie nicht einverstanden sind, sagen Sie:
  Das stimmt nicht.
  Ich bin nicht damit einverstanden.
  Ich bin ganz anderer Meinung.
  Ich muss Ihnen da widersprechen.
  Nach meiner Erfahrung ist das nicht der Fall.

- Um einen Kompromiss zu schließen, sagen Sie:
  Da stimme ich Ihnen zu.
  Das mag sein.
  Das kann sein.

Source: Schauplatz © Brien, Brien, Christie & Schommartz (Heinemann Educational, 2000)

3. Students should next be encouraged to undertake small research tasks during the teaching phase so that they become familiar with the range of materials available to them before choosing their coursework theme, for example, videos to borrow, extracts of newspapers to read. It is essential that the students understand the scope of their coursework topic before choosing it. By learning how to identify and extract information from a range of resources, even if in a superficial way initially, the student can make an informed choice of what is involved and whether he or she will have enough ideas to pursue it. (See checklist in Chapter 2.)

Literature

Traditionally, literature has been taught intensively to enable the student to handle detailed 'context questions' or to write essays under examination conditions. While this form of study has its own rewards, it can at times lead to teacher and student ploughing through a text, trying to master every nuance and obscure turn of phrase. This can lead to students becoming demotivated and it does not inspire creativity.

The use of literature for coursework can be a liberating experience for two reasons. The student always has the text and notes to refer to at leisure, so does not have to learn quotations or references. A thorough knowledge of the whole text is not required as the student will inevitably focus on specific characters or details and the teacher can guide the reading to cover the more interesting or salient points.

Students can be set pages to read in advance and given a whole variety of comprehension exercises to undertake each time. Variety is key as this will maintain student motivation and interest. Listed below are a number of techniques to enable students to improve their comprehension of literature:

- questions in target language with specific reference to characters;
- questions in target language with reference to pages/paragraphs;
- put a list of events in the correct order;
- give students quotes: they have to answer who? in which context? and analyse why this was said;
- as above but with a gapped version of the quotation to be completed;
- grammatical exercises and translation based on the text.

The more the teacher can 'scaffold' the student's reading the better. It is, for example, often helpful to include page number references with questions. This saves the student time and prevents him or her becoming frustrated with trying to find the right place in the book!

Although comprehension of the story/plot is important, it is my view that one should move beyond this as soon as possible. If student and teacher can collaborate on the comprehension stage, they can progress all the more quickly to the analysis stage. In order to obtain the higher marks for coursework, students need to move away from the narrative/descriptive towards the **analytical** and **creative**. There are a number of ways in which this analysis can be done to make it more interesting:

- debates/role plays;
- pairs/groups identify and list key points in text for a particular character;
- dialogues/monologues/letters/e-mails from a character's point of view.

When looking at the topic of 'media', we identified sub-sections for further exploration. These are less easy to specify for literature as they will depend on the work being studied. We can, however, identify some general areas:

- study of one character: motivation, relationships;
- comparison of two characters or character types in the same book or two books, e.g. two mothers;
- discussion of a theme: love, unemployment;
- comparison of two books; comparison of book with the film of the book;
- study of how the book relates to contemporary society, i.e. as an aspect of a topic.

As with the topic, one should give students a feel for all these different approaches to literature during the teaching phase. They should participate in role plays, analysis of parts of the text and identify an area they wish to explore further. This might be done by giving students 'micro-writing' tasks in which they try out different approaches.

Film

The study of film is increasingly popular as teachers recognise how visually literate students have become. It is seen as motivating and relevant and is a rich source of coursework. In addition, of course, film can make the cultural element of coursework very vivid for students.

Once students have seen the film through once, there is a variety of activities one can undertake to make the comprehension phase come alive:

- freeze-frame description/prediction;
- brainstorming adjectives to describe individual characters or scenes;
- viewing with the sound down to focus students on the visual impact of the scene;
- listening: sound only, to focus on listening comprehension;
- listening: sound only, for the presence of a character/the order of events;
- writing summaries in English or the TL;
- translation;
- retranslation;

- proof correction of a script;
- completion/anticipation of the script;
- subtitling;
- grammatical exercises;
- completing dialogues;
- matching dialogue to action;
- sequencing events or extracts of dialogue.

As with literature, one can then move towards more analysis and undertake activities such as role plays and debates. In larger classes, one can divide the class into groups to consider the film(s) from different points of view, perhaps using a critic's words as a stimulus. In their groups, students can then gather evidence from the film to see if they agree or disagree with a critic's analysis.

The aspects of the film a student may choose to focus upon are similar to those listed above under 'literature':

- study of one character: motivation, relationships;
- comparison of two characters or character types in the same film or two films, e.g. two mothers;
- discussion of a theme: love, unemployment;
- comparison of two films sharing the same theme;
- study of how the film relates to contemporary society, i.e. as part of a topic.

It is important that students have the vocabulary necessary to treat a literary or cinematic topic appropriately. Some literary/cinematic vocabulary in French, German and Spanish is provided on pp67, 70 and 76.

Encouraging personal opinions

As we have already noted, it is the **analysis** of the topic, book or film that will be the focus of the coursework and students may need further practice in this before going off to plan their work independently.

One way to direct attention onto this is to devise a communicative oral/micro-writing exercise which shifts the focus from the descriptive/factual to the giving of opinions. Students are shown pictures relating to the topic (e.g. television) and asked to give an oral or written reaction using the following grid. The advantage of such a grid is that it takes the student through the process of description to analaysis and evaluation of the topic. The grid can, of course, be adapted to other contexts.

RESPONDING TO STIMULUS MATERIAL	
Mots-clés	
De quoi s'agit-il? Que voyez-vous?	
Qui?	
Pourquoi? Qu'est-ce qu'on veut communiquer?	
Etes-vous d'accord?	
Réaction personnelle/opinion	
Conséquences pour l'avenir	
D'autres thèmes possibles	
Phrases-clés	

Theme: La télévision

Or perhaps a board game could be used: students advance around a board (see opposite) giving opinions on the topic each time they land on a square. They have to select starter phrases for these opinions from a list of opinion phrases which they have already had presented to them and, preferably, learnt (see below). The winner is the first student to reach the finishing square.

A mon avis ... /Selon moi ...	In my view ...
En ce qui me concerne ...	As far as I'm concerned ...
Je pense/crois/trouve que ...	I think/believe/find that ...
Je soutiens que ...	I maintain that ...
Je suis persuadé(e) que ...	I am convinced that ...
Je suis convaincu(e) que ...	I am convinced that ...
Il est peu probable que...	It is unlikely that ...
Il est incontestable que ...	It is unquestionable that ...
Il me semble que ...	It seems to me that ...
On ne peut pas nier que ...	One cannot deny that ...

German and Spanish equivalent phrases are provided on pp71 and 78.

Students can also be encouraged to write some opinion phrases of their own, a useful source being the centre pages of the large, hardback Collins dictionaries. In addition, they can make their own board games in pairs or small groups. A German and Spanish version are included on pp72 and 78.

On completion of the game, students can write sentences which combine the opinion phrase and the statement, for example, *Il est incontestable que la publicité exploite les femmes.*

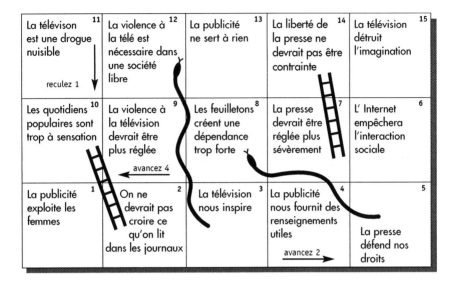

The main purpose of such activities is not so much to teach the language of opinions, as this is an ongoing task from the outset of the course. It is rather to help students appreciate the importance of offering a personal opinion in the context of coursework and to 'kick-start' this process.

Students need to move from the mere **identification** of a body of specialist vocabulary and opinion phrases to making them **their own**. Class debates can generate a great deal of vocabulary use and motivation and provide an authentic stimulus for written work. They personalise the topic and engage students. This is an example of how all classwork is inter-connected. Coursework is not just a focus in itself – everything one does in class in all skill areas contributes to the process of preparing a good piece of coursework.

Here is a format for structuring a debate on the topic of violence on TV where use can be made of the specialist vocabulary above.

Conducting a debate

before

1. Choose a topic of interest and which involves clashes of personality.

2. Issue each student with a summary of the scenario and a role card containing his or her opinion in bullet points.

3. Each student prepares his or her role (notes) and chooses at least one opinion phrase (written down). Stress to the student that he or she needs to develop his or her character as much as possible. Tell students they will be marked for fluency, accuracy and content.

during

1. Brainstorm all relevant vocabulary and phrases and write on board for students to refer to if necessary.

2. Group students in a circle with no desks or books, just their notes. Video the debate where possible to give a sense of urgency.

3. Issue each student with a 'wild card' phrase to be used in the course of debate. This will be an opinion phrase already learnt and can be differentiated according to the ability of each student. The student places the card into the middle of the circle during the debate, once he or she has used the phrase concerned.

4. Each student introduces him or herself in role and outlines his or her argument briefly.

5. Using a set formula, each student names one person he or she agrees with and one person he or she disagrees with, giving reasons, e.g. *Je suis d'accord avec ... parce que ...*

6. Students should now begin to contribute freely. Prompt students who are reluctant to participate and encourage use of (dis)agreement phrases: *Ce n'est pas le cas/Ce n'est pas vrai/Vous vous trompez/Tout à fait ...*

7. Teacher is outside the circle, supporting each speaker with vocabulary if necessary and prompting others to counter, perhaps by offering the beginning of a sentence. Bring debate to a compromise and vote at the end.

after

Give individual feedback where possible, highlighting consistent grammatical mistakes and suggestions for improving content matter. Giving marks for the debate can be motivating and helpful as well.

After the debate, or for homework, students could write it up, perhaps in the form of a newspaper article, giving extensive quotations of each person's arguments. This helps students to include all sides of an argument in their work and is a useful consolidation exercise.

Sample roles:

Mère: pour une censure

- la vie est très chargée; doit laisser ses enfants devant la télévision quand elle est occupée.
- on n'a pas le temps de vérifier si les films sont violents ou pas.
- les enfants ont le droit de regarder la télévision seuls dans la chambre.

Metteur en scène: contre une censure

- doit avoir la possibilité de s'exprimer et de montrer la réalité telle qu'elle est.
- veut montrer la réalité telle qu'elle est.

Chercheur: pour une censure

- la recherche montre que la violence à la télévision incite les gens à devenir violents.
- la violence nuit aux émotions.

Prêtre: pour une censure

- la société doit montrer un exemple morale.
- il faut protéger nos enfants.

Chef d'une chaîne de télévision: contre une censure

- trouve la violence populaire et nécessaire pour le financement de la chaîne.
- pense qu'un avertissement avant un film violent suffit.

Téléspectateur: contre une censure

- pense que les adultes ont le droit de choisir eux-mêmes.
- croit que les parents devraient surveiller leurs enfants de plus près.

Using a variety of resources

We shall look at the research and study required in more detail in Chapter 5. At this stage, it is helpful to emphasise the variety of resources that exist for coursework material. Ask students to brainstorm the sources in pairs or groups, making sure that they home in on the TL culture/country. This is a good opportunity to direct them away from English resources and ones that are too general and make no reference to the country being studied.

The following can be used as a checklist to help students see how many different types of resources they have identified.

listening	• to cassettes • to native speakers expressing opinions on a topic • to the radio • to Internet audio files/streamed broadcasts	**watching**	• commercially produced videos • authentic TV programmes • a film • video clips on the Internet
reading	• magazine articles • newspaper articles • textbooks/coursebooks • supplementary reading materials: *Authentik, Etincelle*, etc. • government booklets/leaflets • surveys		• literature from political groups/pressure groups • Internet texts • transcripts of native speaker comments • other books • e-mails/letters to/from native speakers

Clearly, not all these sources will be available for each topic but the process does set the students thinking on how they are going to gather and then make use of information.

• Teach a general topic/a book/a film and allow scope for the student to define a narrower area of interest within it.
• Allow students the opportunity to develop topic-specific vocabulary.
• Help students with comprehension so they are in a position to move on quickly to analysis.
• Focus students on the processes and necessity of giving personal opinions and identifying a variety of resources.

Research and study skills

Identifying resources

Once a topic and title have been identified, it is essential that resources are also carefully selected and are accessible.

It is often too large and unfocused a task to ask students to research their own resources from scratch without guidance from the teacher. Each resource has to meet several criteria. It must:

- be relevant to the particular aspect of the topic being studied;
- have an appropriate level of language;
- be a reliable and reasonably up-to-date source;
- be unbiased and objective – or clear how and why a one-sided argument is being put.

While an experienced teacher can evaluate a source against the above criteria perhaps at a glance, a student will need to understand the text first before being able to begin evaluating it. After investing a significant amount of time in this process, he or she may well end up having to reject it anyway. Even worse, he or she may proceed with the text, only to realise later that it contained the wrong information or was too hard or basic for coursework purposes.

There is the added complication that a student may well have to plough through a large number of resources to find a small percentage which meets his or her needs. As a teacher, I have had to work hard with colleagues to assemble a decent collection of resources on a topic over a long period. The student rarely has the time or the ability to assemble his or her own resources from scratch and use of the Internet does not necessarily make this task much easier. Many of us have probably spent time surfing the Net for particular, elusive pieces of information. This is hard enough in our own language, when we know exactly what we are looking for.

My point is not that it is impossible for students to identify their own resources. It is rather that it is probably not an efficient use of time, especially when the latter is in short supply and the student is under pressure. In addition, there is the risk that either the student will put off the task, daunted by its enormity, or will become demotivated by the search alone.

In my view, the best way forward is for the teacher – or even better the department as a whole – to assemble a file of resources over time. It will, however, be necessary to monitor that students do not all use the same materials from this file and that they use a good selection. The easiest way of doing this is for students to fill in a tick grid of the resources they are using.

Here is a sample list of resources I have used to teach the topic referred to earlier, that of TV in German:

- compilation video of German TV advertisements;
- TV documentary on the addictive nature of TV;
- article on the way soap operas are constructed;
- clips of German TV soaps;
- listening material on why people watch TV;
- articles on violence on TV, including religious material;
- Government booklet offering advice on children and TV viewing;
- TV schedules from magazines;
- general booklets and articles on the 'mass media'.

It will be noted that the above list contains different media, not simply reading materials. This topic has been a successful one because students can relate it to their own experience and have a variety of sources to which to refer. They do not become bored with simply reading long texts. The teacher should try to incorporate different types of resource into topic work as far as possible, perhaps using the list below as a guide:

- commercially available videos;
- videos of authentic TV broadcasts;
- commercially available listening material;
- recordings of radio broadcasts;
- textbooks (all skill areas);
- newspaper and magazine articles;
- opinions of native speakers at home or abroad, recorded or noted by oneself;
- cassettes/e-mails/videos/transcripts;
- texts or pictures from the Internet.

Getting hold of a variety of materials such as those named above can require a certain degree of resourcefulness. Some were picked up on visits abroad by myself, others sent by German teaching colleagues, others came from textbooks or other commercially produced publications and yet others were contributed by our Swiss foreign language assistant. The more teamwork involved the better and it is helpful if you can ask colleagues or friends in the TL country to keep an eye on the TV/radio schedules for you for items relating to one particular topic! In a larger department it might be possible to ask people to be responsible for gathering information on a couple of topics each. Obviously, the longer one has to collect material the better. While materials will need updating, it is amazing how quickly one can amass a respectable collection of resources. It is helpful to compile files of useful resources so that students can refer to these but it is equally important to keep the originals safe! The main drawback of resource-based learning is that files can easily go astray or become incomplete. It is wise to keep them in the Learning Resources Centre or in a cabinet in a main teaching room and for them to be signed out by students. It is also helpful for teacher and student alike if an up-to-date contents list is maintained as this preserves one's sanity when trying to locate different resources for different students!

Use of English resources should be avoided. They encourage students to undertake spontaneous prose translation which often ends in confused renditions and poor style. In some cases, students may also be encouraged to be too ambitious with their ideas as a result of having read an English text. Some teachers favour the use of English texts in order to provide students with background ideas and some opinions. This is obviously a personal decision but my experience is that the use of English can be counterproductive, a point often mentioned by examiners in their feedback.

A list of useful supplementary resources for research is given in Appendix 3, p69, Appendix 4, p72 and Appendix 5, p78.

Useful French Internet search engines and websites are given below. German and Spanish sites are given in Appendices 4 and 5, pp73 and 79.

Search engines:

(www.google.fr)   (www.lokace.com)

(www.yahoo.fr)   (www.nomade.fr)

Newspapers:

(www.liberation.fr)   (www.lemonde.fr)

(**www.tv5.org**)

This site, provided by TV5, has video clips and songs to download, complete with transcripts. Some worksheets are also available to download.

(**www.bva.fr**) (**www.ifop.fr**)

Sites which publish the results of French opinion polls. Ideal for facts and statistics.

(**www.radio-france.fr**)

Excellent for reading and listening to Radio France reports on topical issues.

(**www.sidaweb.com**)

Useful for research on the topic of AIDS.

(**www.momes.net**)

A fascinating site on which young people can post an opinion on a whole variety of subjects. Students can use the material to stimulate their own ideas and to obtain invaluable phrases and vocabulary. You need to find your way to the *Forum: Correspondants > Forum*.

Various languages:

(**www.euronews.net**)

The latest news in French, German, Spanish, Italian, Portuguese and Russian.

(**www.modlangs.co.uk**) (subscription payable)

Offers a variety of services, for French, German and Spanish, for example: *Feline:* weekly printable sheets on current news topics and *Felinx:* interactive on-screen exercises.

(**www.channel4.com/amazinggrades**) (subscription payable)

Links to sites which are researched, reviewed and updated.

Another invaluable source of material is an exchange visit abroad. Before the visit, students should be asked to draw up a survey or questionnaire relating to the coursework topic concerned. It might relate to attitudes to the environment, television viewing habits, a critique of a film and so on. Exchange students can be encouraged to write a short critique of a film or book being studied and this can be used as a reference source for coursework writing.

If an exchange visit abroad is not feasible, students should still try to keep in regular contact with a penfriend abroad who can be a useful source of material. Contact can be by letter or, even better, by e-mail. The penfriend could not only send relevant articles but be canvassed for his or her views on a variety of issues.

Michael Evans, Linda Fisher and Edith Esch at Cambridge University Faculty of Education have set up the TIC-TALK project. This uses computer-mediated conferencing as a means of enhancing cultural awareness. The project co-ordinators paste contemporary, possibly controversial, photographs on a bulletin board with a few questions. This is designed to provoke a response from both English and French pupils in a discussion forum, giving both sets of students access to up-to-date target language material. Contact **mje1000@hermes.cam.uk** for further details.

Even if one does not have the technology, money or time to participate in this type of project, it should still be possible to set up an e-mail discussion with a partner school.

Note-taking

Once a student has identified an appropriate text on which to work, the next stage is to take notes so that the information gained can be incorporated into the piece of coursework. From one text, the student will need to make different types of notes so that it can be exploited to the full:

- basic notes on content, summarising main points, including any statistics;
- items of specialised vocabulary;
- phrases which can be adapted which relate to the specific topic;
- quotations which can be used to support a point;
- phrases of a general nature which can be used when introducing arguments, opinions, etc.

This could be set out by the student in grid form (see overleaf):

Contenu: points principaux, statistique

Vocabulaire

Phrases (thème)

Citations

Phrases générales

It can be helpful to underline relevant words/phrases or highlight them in a different colour at first. Exercises can be done in class on note-taking to help students get to grips with this skill and help them focus on taking notes in a concise way. Students are often tempted to copy whole chunks of a passage for fear of missing anything vital. This not only constitutes plagiarism and is not permitted but also often leads to irrelevant material being included.

Various exercises in reading can be practised in order to hone students' note-taking skills:

■ Reading a text at speed in pairs and summarising it in one sentence;

■ Underlining or highlighting in different ways:
  – words they know
  – words they can guess
  – words they do not need to know
  – words they need to look up;

■ Matching headings to each paragraph of a text and also writing their own headings;

■ Re-ordering sentences, supplied by the teacher, which summarise a text and then writing their own ten-sentence summary;

■ Picking out the most relevant quotation which sums up a text;

■ Picking out and listing topic-specific or key vocabulary;

■ Picking out and listing generic/multi-use phrases.

Advanced Pathfinder 2: Developing learning strategies (Jones 2001) provides useful guidance on all aspects of study skills, including note-taking.

The following grid is useful for helping students to take notes from and analyse radio/television news items or other programmes which may pertain to their area of study: German and Spanish versions of this grid are provided on p73 and p80.

INFORMATIONS

1 – Regardez/Ecoutez bien les informations et complétez la grille:

Info	Qui?	Où?	Quand?	Quoi?	Comment?	Combien?	Pourquoi?

2 – Pour chaque information, écrivez les mots-clés.

The following exercise is an example of one which can be used to help students gather topic-specific vocabulary:

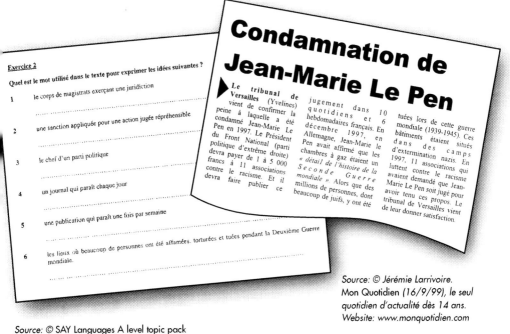

Exercice 2

Quel est le mot utilisé dans le texte pour exprimer les idées suivantes ?

1 le corps de magistrats exerçant une juridiction

2 une sanction appliquée pour une action jugée répréhensible

3 le chef d'un parti politique

4 un journal qui paraît chaque jour

5 une publication qui paraît une fois par semaine

6 les lieux où beaucoup de personnes ont été affamées, torturées et tuées pendant la Deuxième Guerre mondiale.

Condamnation de Jean-Marie Le Pen

▶ Le tribunal de Versailles (Yvelines) vient de confirmer la peine à laquelle a été condamné Jean-Marie Le Pen en 1997. Le Président du Front National (parti politique d'extrême droite) devra payer de 1 à 5 000 francs à 11 associations contre le racisme. Et il devra faire publier ce jugement dans 10 quotidiens et 6 hebdomadaires français. En décembre 1997, en Allemagne, Jean-Marie Le Pen avait affirmé que les chambres à gaz étaient un « détail de l'histoire de la Seconde Guerre mondiale ». Alors que des millions de personnes, dont beaucoup de juifs, y ont été tuées lors de cette guerre mondiale (1939-1945). Ces bâtiments étaient situés dans des camps d'extermination nazis. En 1997, 11 associations qui luttent contre le racisme avaient demandé que Jean-Marie Le Pen soit jugé pour avoir tenu ces propos. Le tribunal de Versailles vient de leur donner satisfaction.

Source: © Jérémie Larrivoire.
Mon Quotidien (16/9/99), le seul quotidien d'actualité dès 14 ans.
Website: www.monquotidien.com

Source: © SAY Languages A level topic pack

This one encourages them to collect statistics:

---

4 Was passt zusammen?

Welche Zahlen passen zu welchen Sätzen? Sehen Sie
sich den Bericht noch einmal an, um zu prüfen, ob Sie
Recht haben.

a 1.800 Meter	1 Die Länge des Staus bei Graz. ☐
c 16 Kilometer	3 Die Höhe der Autobahn am Brenner-Pass. ☐
d 60	4 Die Zahl der Radarpistolen. ☐
e 40 Kilometer	5 Die Zahl der Baustellen auf den Autobahnen in Österreich. ☐

Source: TV Aktuell © M. McAleavy (OUP, 2000)

Use of these exercises at various intervals will not only help improve students'
reading comprehension skills overall but provide them with important tools for
tackling coursework texts.

Quotations from a book or film are good to use and give a flavour of the source
material but need to be used sparingly and it is important that they support a point
as precisely as possible. Students can compile lists of key points and key
quotations in class to make this task easier when they come to select material for
their coursework. All quotations must be clearly attributed in the final piece and
it should be remembered that they are not included in the overall word-count.

Plagiarism

Students also need to be advised on avoiding plagiarism. Not only is it against
exam board regulations and often instantly recognisable but in most cases it
lowers the quality of the piece of work. This is because the student is probably
using a passage out of context, in an inappropriate register. OCR regulations, for
example, state that students should not use more than six words from a text,

otherwise they must be attributed as a quotation. They should also be made aware that this includes the following:

- translating from English texts;

- copying word for word or adapting whole sections/paragraphs/pages, even if some changes have been made. This includes material from the Internet, of course;

- asking native speakers or others to check or correct work.

Students must, of course, learn to use some phrases, in adapted form, for their coursework, otherwise they will never be able to assimilate more complex vocabulary and structures. Exercises which encourage students to manipulate and adapt text are not only useful for the final exam but also help them produce better coursework.

Exercises may involve any of the following:

1. Text manipulation: asking students to rephrase a sentence using a different structure, for example:

   Il ne faut pas manger des frites becomes *Les frites ne doivent ...*

   A son avis les prix sont trop hauts becomes *Il ...*

   Notre départ est prévu pour 16 heures becomes *Nous allons ...*

2. Transfer of meaning from English into the target language using phrases from a given target language text.

3. Finding synonyms for words underlined.

4. Rewriting parts of a text in the target language and asking students to locate the original in a given text. Students can then rewrite other parts themselves.

Students should keep a careful note of the sources they use as these all need to be listed in the bibliography at the end of their piece of coursework. They should also note specific references for their quotations as all quotations need to be acknowledged.

One must not forget the use of other reference works when writing coursework. A good A level vocabulary book can provide invaluable specialist vocabulary. This can be used pro-actively, i.e. a student can be encouraged to plan specifically to incorporate certain terms rather than just consulting the vocabulary lists when necessary.

The following extract from an A level vocabulary book shows items of vocabulary usefully grouped together for ease of reference.

EL ALCOHOL

el abstemio	*teetotaller*
el alcohólico	*alcoholic*
el alcoholímetro	*Breathalyser ®*
el alcoholismo	*alcoholism*
alcoholizar	*to alcoholise*
la bebida alcohólica	*alcoholic drink*
el borracho *(inf)*	*drunk*
el copeo/chateo *(inf)*	*pub crawl*

ebrio	*intoxicated*
la embriaguez	*drunkenness*
estar borracho	*to be drunk*
estar trompa *(inf)*	*to be stoned*
la excitabilidad	*excitability*
la intoxicación alcohólica	
	alcohol poisoning
la resaca	*hangover*
sobrio	*sober*
vomitar	*to be sick*

inducir a alguien a la bebida	*to drive somebody to drink*
bajo los efectos del alcohol	*under the influence of alcohol*
si bebes no conduzcas	*don't drink and drive*
0,8 ml de alcohol en la sangre	*0.8 ml of alcohol in the blood*
darse a la bebida	*to go on the booze*
estar como una cuba *(inf)*	*to be stoned*
el abuso del alcohol entre los jóvenes	*excessive drinking amongst the young*

Source: Advanced Spanish Vocabulary © I. Melero Orta (Nelson Thornes, 2001)

key points

- Compile a resource bank for each topic, drawing on as large a variety of media as possible.
- Offer students strategies and guidelines for taking notes.
- Ensure students understand the rules regarding plagiarism.
- Encourage students to develop ways of expressing facts in their own words and being pro-active in the use of topic-specific vocabulary.

5

Planning the coursework

Once a student has selected an area of study for coursework, he or she then has to determine how exactly to approach the planning.

As with the choice of topic in the first place, it is useful if the student chooses an aspect that has a personal perspective, either because the student can relate his or her own experience to it or because it involves personalities with whom he or she can empathise. This not only increases motivation but also means the student is likely to have a foundation on which to develop opinions. Some examples of how a topic can be personalised are shown below:

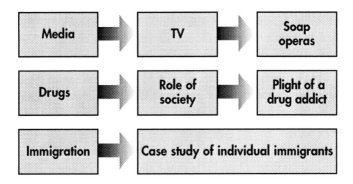

Literary or film characters can also be used to add a personal dimension.

The teacher will obviously play a key role in this decision and help the student choose an appropriate topic (as outlined in Chapter 3), possibly using the checklist featured in Appendix 2.

Types of coursework

The next decision the student has to make is what type of coursework to write, discursive or creative.

Students sometimes view a creative piece as an easy option. In many cases, creative writing is more demanding than the discursive option. Creative writing should demonstrate the same degree of organisation, development and knowledge but has the added complication that it needs to be written in a convincing style. It may involve expressing oneself in the style of a literary character or writing in the style of a tabloid newspaper. This is a skill which can be hard to acquire in a foreign language for some students.

Literature and/or film provides a good basis for creative coursework. The suggestions below are possible forms it could take:

• a newspaper article including facts from various sources, perhaps focusing on a character from a book;

• a letter to the author of a book – in some cases this can be a reply to an author's stated intentions;

• a letter from one character to another, or a diary extract, justifying actions. The context can be set by referring to a particular point/incident in the book/film when the letter/extract is being written.

Similar pieces can be written for topic work where there can be a focus on an individual character, for example, the problems of an immigrant through the eyes of one or two individuals or a study of the inner cities from the point of view of a film character, for example, in *La haine*.

Choosing a title

A clear, focused title can make all the difference between an average piece of coursework and a good one. A well-chosen title forces the student to address the criteria of relevance, organisation and development as the piece will demand a logical progression and structure. It is very tempting for students to write extensively and knowledgeably on a topic but for it to be rambling and unfocused. The title might as well be, for example, 'Everything I know about racism in France.' Students have often tried to persuade me to let them choose a title *after* they have finished the coursework so that they can fit the title to what they have written. This is to be avoided as it always ends up as a compromise. It is far better to encourage the student to focus early on and then select only the material that answers the question.

One should not be afraid of long coursework titles. Sometimes a long title is necessary to make clear to the reader what is being addressed. Examples are:

- 'Analyse the character of the mother in … In what respect is she responsible for her daughter's downfall?'

- 'How objective do you find the character's accounts of events in …?'

- 'Who is responsible for … and why? Could her plight have been avoided?'

- 'Has advertising in … gone too far?'

- 'What are the effects of TV violence on the public and should controls on TV violence be tighter?'

- 'Do soap operas serve a useful purpose for TV channels and the public?'

Note how these titles have a precise focus and require specific responses. (In each case, it is taken for granted that the focus will be the TL country/culture and this is not spelt out.) This will help shift the student's response away from the descriptive towards the analytical. Such titles should generally give rise to better coursework than vaguer ones such as 'Violence on Spanish TV' or 'The character of the mother in … '.

Here are some guidelines for choosing a title:

DO

☑ Pose a specific question.

☑ Use question words such as 'Why?', 'How?', 'What are the effects of … ?'

☑ Ask the student to **analyse**.

☑ Encourage two-part (but linked) questions if there is not enough material/ideas to answer one question.

☑ Limit the scope of the question where it helps to focus it more: 'A comparison of tabloid and broadsheet newspapers with particular reference to …'

DON'T

☒ Use words such as 'describe'.

☒ Allow all-encompassing titles like 'The Environment'.

☒ Formulate a question so narrowly that the student does not have enough ideas – broaden it into two questions or aspects.

It is tempting to allow titles such as 'The Environment' or 'Racism in ...' because one is afraid that the student will otherwise not have enough to write. My experience is that a student often includes too much, following the old adage: '*If you fire enough ammunition, you are bound to hit something*'. Focusing the title actually encourages the student to select resources, think out implications of the title and frees him or her up to express personal opinions – all of which will gain him or her more marks.

Here are some clearly focused titles quoted from the Edexcel coursework guide:

'*Les mesures prises contre la pollution en France ont-elles été efficaces?*'

'*Un film de Truffaut ...: jusqu'à quel point est-il autobiographique?*'

Below is an exercise for students to do in order to help them write focused titles:

Ecrivez des titres plus précis:

1. *Les problèmes de l'Union Européenne.*
2. *Les drogues en France.*
3. *La violence dans les collèges.*
4. *Une étude de Paris.*
5. *L'immigration.*

Schreiben Sie genauere Titel:

1. *Der Euro.*
2. *Die Umwelt.*
3. *Die Neo-Nazis in Deutschland.*
4. *Berlin seit dem Fall der Mauer.*
5. *Tourismus in Österreich.*

Escriba títulos más claros:

1. *Un estudio de Madrid.*
2. *La cuestión de Gibraltar.*
3. *La Guerra Civil.*
4. *La obra de Pablo Picasso.*
5. *El medioambiente.*

Writing a plan

Obviously, plans will differ depending on the subject matter of the piece of coursework but the application of some general principles will help keep the piece as focused as possible.

It is good to use target language terminology as this can then be included in the final plan. Here is a suggested format for a plan. This can only serve as a general template but can still form a useful basis for a student's planning.

Einleitung/Introduction/Introducción
A summary of what will be discussed and why it is of interest/significance.

Teil 1/Section 1/1° parte
An outline of the issue: probably mainly factual. May include a definition of terms in the title.

Teil 2/Section 2/2° parte
A survey of one point of view (the opposite of the writer's own) with supporting evidence and quotations.

Teil 3/Section 3/3° parte
A survey of one's own point of view with supporting evidence and quotations.

Teil 4/Section 4/4° parte
An indication of how things may change in the future/how things might have been different.

Schluss/Conclusion/Conclusión
A brief summary of both points of view, with the accent on own view. Possibly finish with an important quotation to support one's point, or a pertinent question.

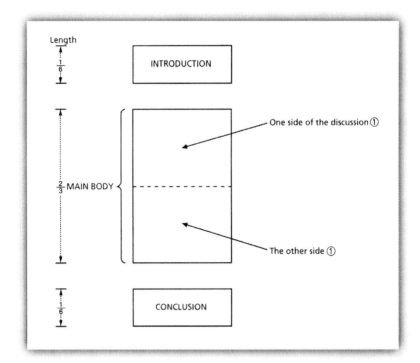

Source: Compal 2000 © Hares & Elliott (Hodder and Stoughton, 1997)

It is just as vital to plan well for a piece of **creative** coursework. A letter from a character in a book, for example, will need to deal with certain events in that book and show evidence of development and organisation.

Here are some points to consider including in a piece of creative coursework such as a letter from one character in a book to another. It mirrors the plan for a topic-based piece of coursework:

- Reason for writing the letter;

- Reference to events which take place in the book and other characters' interpretation(s) of them;

- Suggestions of how events will develop/how things could have been different;

- A summary of the points made, possibly ending with questions to be answered in the reply.

The writing of the plan is a crucial part of the execution of coursework and one in which the teacher has important input. The plan should be as comprehensive as possible (but not more than one side of A4), breaking down each section into detailed sub-sections. If the outline for each paragraph is carefully given in the plan, the teacher and student alike can be confident that the execution of the final piece will be more successful. The teacher is allowed to work closely with the student on the plan, giving advice and offering suggestions. Once the plan has been agreed, no further involvement of the teacher is allowed.

Although students are not permitted to submit drafts of their actual coursework, it is good for them to undertake a piece of practice coursework, focusing on planning. This can follow on from a topic studied as a whole class, with each student being set the same title. They can then work in pairs or groups, where appropriate, to plan the essay. The class as a whole can come to a decision as to which would be the best plan. This exercise can also be carried out to decide upon a good title, with students perhaps being given a selection and ranking them from the best to the worst. The plans overleaf are original examples of work by students from Newham Sixth Form College.

Titre:
L'immigration de l'après-guerre en France, à qui a-t-elle profité? Aux immigrés ou à la France?

PLAN

L'introduction
- Expliquer la question
- Définir l'immigration
- Statistiques

1ère partie:
- Après la seconde guerre mondiale
- Chiffres
- Raisons
- Qui a bénéficié?

2ème partie:
- Les conditions d'accueil
- Logement
- Travail
- Qui a bénéficié?

3ème partie:
- La situation aujourd'hui
- Racisme
- Problèmes

4ème partie:
- Les exemples de réussite

Conclusion
Nous avons bénéficié tous ...

The above plan gives a clearly focused title, specifying the precise topic and timescale and posing an unambiguous question. Each section is then broken down into discrete sections. There is scope for more detail in the plan but the main aim of the plan is to give an overall structure and to organise material coherently. A lot of detail in the plan is not always required if the student is clear in his or her own mind what he or she is going to write for each section. A plan that is too wordy can sometimes detract from a sharp focus for the piece.

Titre:

'Déesses d'amour ou déesses de destruction? *Les belles dames sans merci* de François Truffaut.'

PLAN

Partie A: La femme magique
- La signification de la femme magique dans les films et les arguments principaux qui l'entourent.
- L'élément autobiographique.
- Le mélange d'hostilité et d'attraction envers la femme magique.
- Catherine – la déesse définitive de Truffaut.
- Les conflits turbulents entre les sentiments humains et l'identité surhumaine.

Partie B: La femme fatale
- La récompense morbide d'une femme trompée – Julie Kohler, la meurtrière sans merci.
- L'adultère fatale – le cas de Franca Lachenay.
- Existe-t-il une justification romantique pour cette vengéance?

Partie C: L'amour fait mal – les relations entre les deux sexes
- Les différences de comportement entre les deux sexes.
- La folie fondamentale de l'homme dans les films.
- Est-ce que c'est possible pour une femme d'être séduisante et peu conventionnelle sans être un assassin monstrueux? – *La femme d'à côté* par opposition à *La nuit américaine*.

La conclusion

This plan does offer more detail and breaks the material down into three clear sections, although the student may have found it useful to spell out some ideas for the introduction and conclusion. The title is, once again, clearly focused.

key points
- Ideally, a chosen topic should have a personal perspective to it.
- The student should be as pro-active as possible at the planning stage, working closely with the teacher.
- The student needs to choose a clearly focused title.
- The plan should be as detailed as possible and agreed with the teacher.

6

Writing and reviewing

We have noted how vital it is to have a comprehensive, accurate and relevant plan approved by the teacher. It is then important that the student understands that the plan is not a separate exercise in itself but that it should be followed, as far as possible, to the letter! It has been known for students to go away and produce a piece of coursework which is totally different from the agreed plan! It may even be worth asking students to tick off each point as it is covered in the piece of work. Students could also run through a final checklist before the writing actually begins:

My coursework:

☐ ... has a sharply focused title.

☐ ... has a detailed plan, agreed with my teacher.

☐ ... deals with the target-language country/culture.

☐ ... uses a number of target-language source materials.

Once the student has his or her plan and has understood which sections of the essay will cover which points, he or she needs to ensure that paragraphs within the essay are constructed as well as possible. Generally, paragraphs will follow a structure like this:

- An opening sentence to summarise the content of the paragraph. This signposting is for the reader.
- A statement of one's point/argument.
- An example/quotation/statistic to back up or illustrate one's point with a concrete reference.
- A final sentence to round off or bring home one's point/argument.

Such a structure avoids a paragraph becoming a jumbled collection of thoughts and points and also helps a student confine each paragraph to a specific point. This should also be applied to creative work as far as possible to give it a clear focus and progression.

Study the example paragraph below and see if you can isolate the five basic components.

Mais ce qui m'a frappé le plus en Belgique n'a rien à voir avec les livres, le café, ou le rire. C'est en fait votre tolérance. Bien sûr que vous vous irritez et que vous vous emportez facilement à un niveau superficiel, mais dans votre for intérieur, vous démontrez une tolérance exemplaire, surtout sur le plan de la race. Les Noirs chez vous, ce sont les Noirs—rien de plus, rien de moins. Serait-ce le fait que vous vous êtes bien installés au carrefour des nations? Quels que soient vos mobiles, vous avez une leçon à nous apprendre.

They are:

1 *The main point*
La chose qui m'a frappé le plus ... c'est en fait votre tolérance.

2 *The explanation*
Vous démontrez une tolérance exemplaire, surtout sur le plan de la race.

3 *The example*
Les Noirs chez vous, ce sont les Noirs—rien de plus, rien de moins.

4 *The personal standpoint*
Quels que soient vos mobiles, vous avez une leçon à nous apprendre.

5 *The context*
Serait-ce le fait que vous vous êtes bien installés au carrefour des nations?

Source: Compol 2000 © Hares & Elliott (Hodder and Stoughton, 1997)

Using a checklist

As a student writes, he or she can make good use of a specialist vocabulary book. As noted earlier, it is best if the student can use the book to help ensure some specialist vocabulary is included as he or she goes along rather than just use it as a reference book to look up words as required. This is a way for a student to monitor that he or she is including a varied lexis in his or her writing, thus satisfying the assessment criteria.

Students can also be given a list of structures to use in their writing to ensure variation. Clearly the list will vary from language to language but could include those below:

- Use of the passive voice;
- Use of subordinate clauses, with some conjunctions specified;
- Use of the conditional (*si/wenn/si*);
- Use of the subjunctive (French);
- Use of reported speech (German).

Barry Jones, in CILT Advanced Pathfinder 2, *Developing learning strategies*, suggests providing students with a list of *charnières* to include in their writing. This adds a level of complexity which the student can monitor him or herself. German and Spanish equivalents of the following expressions are provided in the above book.

mais	d'ailleurs	au reste
et	du moins	autrement
car	néanmoins	de plus
aussi	puis	ensuite
ce qui, ce que	en revanche	ou
cependant	or	pour autant
d'autre part	pourtant	sinon
en effet	par ailleurs	toutefois
en outre	par contre	au surplus
encore	par conséquent	d'un autre côté
également	au contraire	de son côté

Exercises like the following will help students to improve their own written style:

Vokabeln und Strukturen aufbessern

Lesen Sie den folgenden Text und ersetzen Sie die einfachen Vokabeln (unterstrichen) mit den Ausdrücken im Kästchen:

Stichwort Jugendkriminalität

Was steckt dahinter? Tägliche Berichte in den Zeitungen über jugendliche Kriminelle bestätigen die Meinung, dass die neue Generation kriminell ist. Meinungen wie: "Die gehören in den Steinbruch!" sind bei Gesprächen über dieses Problem aktuell.

Jugendkriminalität gibt es, weil es zu wenig Klubs und Aktivitäten gibt. Das ist wahrscheinlich nicht ganz unwahr. Doch steht dem entgegen, was zum Beispiel Burkhard S., Lehrer an einer Rostocker Schule sagt: "Wir versuchen, den Kindern interessante Angebote zu machen.

Aber gerade von den Älteren bekommen wir nur allzu oft zu hören: 'Keinen Bock!' Das treibt den Schweiß."

Im Kindernotdienst der Stadtmission in Evershagen hört man andere Gründe für kriminelles Verhalten bei Kids.

Frau Hannelore Meyer, stellvertretende Leiterin des Heimes, erzählt über ihre Kinder, die fast alle aus problematischen Elternhäusern kommen: "Sie haben oftmals kein Vertrauen in die Erwachsenen. Sie haben Schlimmes gesehen. Die Eltern arbeiten viel oder trinken viel, weil sie ihre Probleme nicht lösen. Die Kinder werden vergessen."

Schützlinge stürzen sich in die Arbeit Reizthema Tatverdächtige bemühen uns bewältigen von der Hand zu weisen Pressemeldungen berichtet wird oft damit erklärt, dass verbirgt sich erlebt ergeben sich dem Alkohol an der Tagesordnung bleiben dabei auf der Strecke ausnahmslos gestörten heranwachsende Äußerungen Freizeitmöglichkeiten zweifellos erfährt

Source: Schauplatz © Brian, Brian, Christie & Schommartz (Heinemann Educational, 2000)

As writing proceeds, students should be encouraged to use a checklist of common errors to check their work for grammatical accuracy.

WRITING CHECKLIST (French)

1. Have I checked nouns and do they have the correct
   - genders?
   - plurals?

2. Do my adjectives agree?

3. Are my cases correct, especially:
   - direct and indirect object pronouns?

4. Have I used the correct prepositions?

5. Have I checked my verbs?

   - do they agree with the subject?
   - do verbs in the past tense take *avoir/être*?
   - do regular verb forms follow the rules?
   - are irregular verb forms correct?
   - have I avoided mixing tenses?
   - have I used the correct tenses/tense sequence?
   - have I used the subjunctive with conjunctions/constructions which take it?
   - have I used the infinitive where necessary?

German and Spanish versions are given in the Appendices on pp74 and 81.

It is even better if students can use a personal list which they have compiled during their course to date. If, as and when they receive corrected work back, they note particular areas of weakness, they can use this list as a focus for their corrections. Such a list may look like this:

- *adjective endings, especially in the dative*
- *word order after 'weil'*
- *verb agreements in the present tense*
- *verbs in the perfect taking 'sein'*
- *'könnte' not 'konnte' in the conditional*

Students will also have compiled their own list of useful essay phrases. Initially, this will have come from the teacher and can then be personalised. Overleaf is a list of useful French phrases; see pp75 and 81 for German and Spanish versions.

Etant donné/vu que …	Given that …
Advienne que pourra …	Come what may …
Il est certain que …	It is certain that …
Il se pourrait bien que …	It could be that …
Rien ne permet de penser que …	There is no reason to believe that …
Il faut constater que …	It must be said that …
Cela a pour conséquence que …	This results in …
La société actuelle ne devrait pas tolérer …	Modern society should not tolerate …
Il est révélateur que …	It is significant that …
D'une part …, d'autre part …	On the one hand, … on the other …
On considère à juste titre …	People rightly think …

In addition, phrases for specific purposes such as talking about statistics, are invaluable and should be learned:

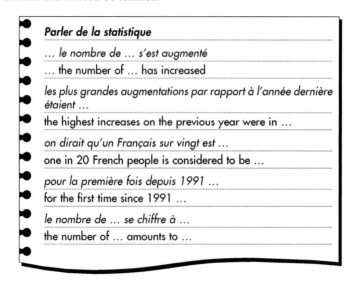

Parler de la statistique

… le nombre de … s'est augmenté
… the number of … has increased

les plus grandes augmentations par rapport à l'année dernière étaient …
the highest increases on the previous year were in …

on dirait qu'un Français sur vingt est …
one in 20 French people is considered to be …

pour la première fois depuis 1991 …
for the first time since 1991 …

le nombre de … se chiffre à …
the number of … amounts to …

(German and Spanish versions can be found on pp75 and 82.)

Students should be advised to leave their work for a few days after it is finished and then re-read it. If they do this, they should come to it with fresh eyes and spot mistakes and omissions more easily. They can use the checklist on the following page as an overall check.

COURSEWORK: A FINAL CHECK

Check that you can obtain the highest marks possible in each assessed area:

Vocabulary

Have I tried to use unusual words appropriately and specialist ones related to the topic? . . . . ☐
Have I tried to use synonyms? . . . . ☐
(or have I just kept repeating basic, common words?)

Range of expression

Have I used:

Have I varied: . . . .
- linking words? . . . . ☐
- the passive? . . . . ☐
- the conditional? . . . . ☐
- the subjunctive? . . . . ☐
- subordinate clauses? . . . . ☐
- written accents properly? . . . . . ☐
- tenses? . . . . ☐
- word order? (German) . . . . . . ☐
- lengths of sentences? . . . . ☐
- the personal *a* where necessary? (Spanish) . . . . ☐
- verbs like *gustar/encantar* correctly? (Spanish) . . . . ☐
Have I **begun** sentences with a subordinate clause? (German) . . . . ☐
(or have I just used simple sentence structures to play safe?)

Accuracy

Have I honestly **checked** my work several times? . . . . ☐
(or have I just hoped it's right?)
Have I checked:
- tenses to see if subject
  and verb agree? . . . . ☐
- irregular verbs? . . . . ☐
- adjective endings? . . . . ☐
- cases? (German) . . . . ☐
- word order? (German) . . . . . . ☐
Have I read my work critically to see that it makes sense? . . . . ☐

Structure

Have I grouped my ideas together, dealing with each one in turn? . . . . ☐
(or have I just lumped them all together?)
Is there an introduction and conclusion? . . . . ☐

Relevance

Have I answered the question/task requirement? . . . . ☐
(or have I just written down everything I know and hoped it answers the question somehow, somewhere?!)

Examples

Do I give factual information and clear, concrete examples which support the points I am making? . . . . ☐
(or have I just made wild generalisations and statements?)

checklist

Presentation

In terms of presentation, it is always best to word-process work if possible. This way, mistakes can be rectified much more easily and adjustments made. Students can even re-order or replace whole sections/words, etc. without too much trouble. The look of the final piece will also be greatly improved by word-processing. Although good presentation itself does not attract additional marks, it will have a positive effect and improve the overall impression. Boards will generally insist on work being presented on loose-leaf A4 pages, using one side of the paper and lines of text being double-spaced, with a one-inch margin each side. It should also be remembered that key skills can be claimed for appropriate use of ICT.

The main piece of work must also be accompanied by the following:

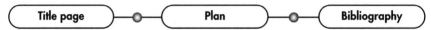

The bibliography should be as full as possible and serves as evidence that wide reading has taken place. Naturally, as wide a range of resources should have been consulted as possible.

Full details of each source should be given, including the precise Web address for Internet material.

It is helpful for students to make use of this tick list before submitting their work:

SUBMISSION OF COURSEWORK: CHECKLIST	✔
I have enclosed my plan.	☐
I have included a title page.	☐
I have only written on one side of the paper.	☐
I have left one-inch margins each side of the paper.	☐
My pages are numbered and in order.	☐
I have attributed all quotations clearly.	☐
I have included a FULL bibliography, including website addresses.	☐
My work is of the required length.	☐
I have checked my work for accuracy.	☐
I have presented my work as neatly and as professionally as possible.	☐

Feedback

Once the first piece of work has been submitted and marked, the teacher is able to offer feedback to the student, in general terms.

While the teacher is not allowed to correct the work or give it back to the candidate, it would be useful to have a tutorial with the student, where time and class numbers allow. The teacher can then highlight areas which need further work, such as verb endings, better organisation of material or greater use of examples. The accompanying feedback sheet (overleaf) could provide a useful focus for this session.

- Encourage students to stick to their plan when writing and to structure paragraphs well.
- Use of a checklist can help students to incorporate a variety of structures in their writing.
- Ask students to check their work carefully, preferably with a gap of a few days after completion.
- General feedback on the first piece of coursework can help to improve performance in the second piece.

Conclusion

The managing of coursework has a variety of aspects and places a number of demands on teacher and student alike.

The teacher needs to organise teaching to incorporate practice of the necessary language and study skills, inspire students to pursue interests in different topic areas, gather together appropriate resources and structure the research and writing process for the student.

The student requires the confidence and perseverance to cope with more independent study over a longer period and the motivation to research new areas of interest and organise his or her time wisely.

The whole process, however, can be extremely rewarding for both, and each teacher and student will be able to develop and refine ways of working which suit their own particular circumstances.

A2 COURSEWORK FEEDBACK

NAME . . . .

TOPIC/TITLE . . . .

KNOWLEDGE AND UNDERSTANDING (Edexcel)/
KNOWLEDGE OF SOCIETY (AQA)/
INFORMATION ABOUT AND UNDERSTANDING OF TOPICS, TEXTS AND
ISSUES (OCR)

ORGANISATION AND DEVELOPMENT OF MATERIAL (Edexcel)/
REACTION/RESPONSE (AQA)

QUALITY OF LANGUAGE (Edexcel, OCR)/
KNOWLEDGE OF GRAMMAR (AQA)

Case studies

Suggested approaches to coursework

Coursework is a very personal undertaking for teacher and student alike and links with personal strengths and interests. A topic or approach which may inspire and motivate one group of students may not work at all with a different group. The teacher may have a particular interest or expertise in literature and be less keen on topic-based work, for example. This will also be an important factor in determining the approaches students will be encouraged to take.

The examples below aim to cover three different types of coursework with examples in a different language each time:

1a Coursework on a topic (drugs) but also with reference to a modern literary text. These examples are in German.
1b Coursework based on literature but with reference to topic-based, background material. These examples are in German.
2 Coursework on a topic (the media) with examples in French.
3 Coursework based around the study of a film with examples in Spanish.

In each case, the context is given with suggestions of suitable types of source material and possible coursework titles. Please note that the titles and topics given are intended as examples only. Students are responsible for providing their own, original titles. Suggested titles are not given for Spanish as areas for exploration are implicit in the text.

Teachers may choose to adopt an approach as it stands or to adapt it to suit their own needs.

1a Literature combined with a topic. Examples in German

Topic: Drugs

The topic area of drugs can be broken down into several aspects as illustrated below:

Students may decide to focus in detail on one particular aspect, illustrating this with examples from a literary text, or may take a wider view, combining several aspects.

Many sources of material are available for teaching and research into this topic:

- coursebooks;
- government booklets aimed at parents and young people;
- information issued by drug rehabilitation centres and organisations;
- articles from a variety of sources.

A survey of German-speaking students will also provide an invaluable source and will help to personalise the work and lend it some originality.

The topic approach can be enriched by combining it with the study of, for example, the book *Wir Kinder vom Bahnhof Zoo*, by Christiane F., the autobiographical story of a young drug addict in Berlin.

The study of the life and character of Christiane F. is very motivating and places the topic of drugs into a real, personal context. Students are then able to write on the topic of drugs using examples from the book to illustrate the social side of the problem.

Suggested coursework titles

1. *Zeitungsartikel: 'Wieviel Drogentote noch?': eine Untersuchung in den Tod eines Mädchens.*
2. *Bericht einer Drogenberaterin: eine Untersuchung des Falls einer Drogensüchtigen und Gründe für ihren Abstieg in die Drogenabhängigkeit.*
3. *Was wird in Deutschland gemacht, um das Drogenproblem zu lösen und wie wirksam sind die Maßnahmen?*
4. *Wer oder was trägt die Hauptverantwortung für das Drogenproblem in Deutschland?*
5. *Wie hilft uns der Fall von Christiane F., das deutsche Drogenproblem zu verstehen?*

1b Comparing two books and using topic-related material as background reading. Examples in German

Topic: Youth Issues, Education, The Role of the Family and Society in Young People's Lives

Literature:

Rolltreppe abwärts, Hans-Georg Noack. A *Jugendroman* about a boy who is put into care after his parents divorce and he is caught shoplifting. It tells the story of his time in a strict children's home and his reactions to his situation.

Wir Kinder vom Bahnhof Zoo, Christiane F. The autobiographical story of a young drug addict in Berlin.

The study of these two books allows interesting comparisons to be made between them: the role of the mother, the issue of responsibility, the objectivity of the accounts, character comparisons. One is fictional, the other autobiographical. There is ample scope for creative writing such as the exchange of letters between characters, the composition of diary entries or the writing of newspaper articles reporting events in the book(s).

Supporting texts and materials can provide useful background reading and topic-specific vocabulary, e.g. textbooks and government booklets for parents on raising a child, contemporary newspaper articles on youth crime.

Suggested coursework titles

Rolltreppe abwärts: *Was sind die Jugendprobleme der modernen deutschen Gesellschaft und wie wirksam sind die Maßnahmen, die eingesetzt werden, um diese Probleme zu überwinden?*

Both books:
1. *Wer trägt die Verantwortung für Jochens und Christianes Situation?*
2. *Hilft die Gesellschaft den Jugendlichen im Buch oder behindert sie sie?*
3. *Analysieren Sie die Einstellungen der Erwachsenen zu den jungen Figuren.*
4. *Ein Vergleich der Rolle der Mutter in den zwei Büchern.*

2   Study of a topic. Examples in French

Topic: Les médias

Sub-topics
La télévision
La presse
La publicité
Les nouveaux médias

The media is an excellent topic for several reasons. It is immediately relevant to students and they can relate to many of the issues. As with the topic of drugs, students may decide to focus on one aspect of the media or take a more general approach. In this case, the former would probably be more focused and more successful as this topic is such a diverse one.

This topic allows students to write generally about television or advertising, for example, but also to analyse individual items. They could discuss the role of soap operas or violence on television, for example, viewing, quoting and analysing specific clips. Advertising offers a rich variety of examples in print, on screen and in audio form. The topic of the press gives students the opportunity to analyse how different newspapers treat a given story or topic. Indeed, students may decide to compare the approaches of different media to a topic.

As mentioned at various points, a personal approach helps motivate students. Surveys of French-speaking students on their viewing/reading/listening habits and attitudes to the media would provide useful data and examples.

Suggested coursework titles

La télévision

1. Expliquez l'importance de la concurrence entre les différentes chaînes de télévision française.
2. Examinez le rôle joué par les feuilletons pour la télévision française et les téléspectateurs.
3. Une analyse de la violence à la télévision française et son effet sur la société.
4. Peut-on tout montrer à la télévision française?

La presse

1. Est-ce que la liberté de la presse est nécessaire?
2. Une comparaison de Libération et France-Soir.

La publicité

1. Une analyse des méthodes de publicité dans trois médias différents.
2. Est-ce que la publicité française nuit à la société?

Le multimédia

Est-ce que le multimédia représente plutôt un risque ou une grande possibilité pour la société française?

3 Study of a film. Examples in Spanish

Film is a valuable tool for stimulating coursework. It can either be used to complement the study of written materials, or perhaps the written materials will complement the film, explaining the issue more clearly.

A useful model for preparing coursework is for students to study a wide-ranging topic as a group. Materials can be provided by the teacher and supplemented by the students. Students with different degrees of interest, commitment or ability will contribute in their different ways. Film fits in well with this pattern, as films and the issues they cover rarely exist in a vacuum. Furthermore, they benefit from group study, as every student's perception of the film and its details will contribute to the collective experience. In large classes, it is quite feasible to have several groups studying different films.

Such an approach will, when it comes to writing coursework, allow students to have the support of the work done as a group, but also to make their own individual decisions about their coursework title and area of interest within the broad topic.

The range of materials will allow students to choose between essays of very differing kinds, ranging from a seriously academic study involving personal research, with the film as formal evidence, through to an imaginative piece of writing in the form of the diary of a character from a film. In the latter case, the film is at the core of the coursework.

This case study looks at the topic of the position of women within Spanish society, which continues to be a significant issue.

As a starting point some suitable resources on women in Spain are these:

- The textbooks *Sigue! 1* and *Sigue! 2* (John Murray) contain suitable materials in various chapters.

- Centres with existing resource banks may find Ian Gibson's BBC video selection called *The Spanish collection*, which has a programme on the topic.

- The collection of materials *Aspectos del mundo hispano* (Advance Materials) has a relevant chapter.

- The Instituto de la Mujer has for years produced relevant material. Much of this can be accessed via the website **www.mas.es** (Ministerio de asuntos sociales).

- Following the Spanish press, particularly via **www.elpais.es** and **www.elmundo.es**, will in a short time produce a range of relevant materials and up-to-date statistics. Teachers or students can provide such articles, which can be studied using the reading grid for news items suggested on p80.

A recent successful film in Spain relates neatly to the topic of women in society. The film is *Solas*, directed by Benito Zambrano and released in 1998. As well as being available on VHS video in Spain, it is issued with English subtitles, and on video and DVD, by Artificial Eye in the UK (**www.artificial-eye.com**), with a 15 certificate.

A careful Internet search will easily reveal a range of good Spanish criticisms on the film. These are valuable linguistically for giving the language to describe events in the film and also for interpretative purposes.

The film was variously reviewed by UK film critics, some of whom clearly and interestingly misunderstood and misjudged it, through their failure to understand the Spanish context.

With or without supporting written material, which may be on the film or on the broader social issues, the film is rich with coursework possibilities. Students may write from the point of view of any one of the characters, or else about the situation of any one of the characters, from an external point of view. Each character is rounded and interesting; each has emotions, hopes and disappointments. Even the wicked father figure has his self-doubts, as he asks his wife whether he has been a good husband.

Other students may prefer to concentrate on the social issues, particularly the rapid generational changes that have occurred in Spain in this respect in little more than 30 years. The film will provide flesh and blood examples to bring the statistics and the sociological conclusions to life.

References

The Spanish collection. BBC (out of print)

Brien, A., Brien, S., Christie, C. and Schommartz, H. (2000) *Schauplatz.* Heinemann Educational.

Connor, J., Jimenez, H. and Mort, D. (2001) *Sigue! 2*, Segunda Edición. John Murray

Connor, J., Jimenez, H., Mort, D. and O'Connor, N. (2000) *Sigue! 1*, Segunda Edición. John Murray

Coursework guide – Edexcel Advanced GCE in German – Issue 1 – August 2000

Deane, M., Popwell, B. and Armstrong, E. (1994) *Au Point.* Nelson

F. Christiane, (1978) *Wir Kinder vom Bahnhof Zoo.* Hamburg: Gruner + Jahr

Frutos-Pérez, M. and Sancho, E. (2000) *Aspectos del mundo hispano: Lectura y puesta en práctica.* Advance Materials

Hares, R. and Elliot, G. (1982) *Compo! 2000.* Hodder and Stoughton

Jones, B (2001) Advanced Pathfinder 2: *Developing learning strategies.* CILT

SAY Languages A level topic pack Immigration A/S

McAleavy, M. (2000) *TV Aktuell.* OUP

Melero Orta I, (1995) *Advanced Spanish Vocabulary.* Nelson Thornes

Noack, H-G (1970) *Rolltreppe abwärts.* Baden-Baden: Signal-Verlag

Sandry, C., Somerville, J., Morris, P. and Aberdeen, H. (2000) *Brennpunkt neue Ausgabe.* Nelson

Appendix 1
Exam board assessment criteria

Chapter 1, p6

AQA

Knowledge of society:
20 marks / 66 $\frac{2}{3}$%

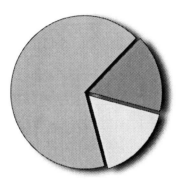

Reaction/Response:
5 marks   16 $\frac{2}{3}$%

Knowledge of grammar:
5 marks   16 $\frac{2}{3}$%

OCR

Information about and
understanding of topics,
texts and issues:
20 marks /66 $\frac{2}{3}$%

Quality of language:
10 marks/33 $\frac{1}{3}$%

The Edexcel breakdown of marks is given on p6.

Appendix 2

Student checklist for a good choice of coursework topic

Chapter 2, p11

✔

- [ ] I can get hold of enough information on the topic in the target language.
- [ ] I am interested enough in this topic to research it fully.
- [ ] The topic is not too general but focuses on one aspect of a broader subject.
- [ ] I can write about the topic in terms of the target-language culture and country.
- [ ] I have some opinions of my own on this topic.
- [ ] There is enough opportunity for me to analyse, not just to describe a story or a situation.
- [ ] This topic allows me to take a creative approach if I want.
- [ ] My teacher will have enough information about the topic to guide me.
- [ ] I have not dealt with (will not deal with) this topic in my other piece of coursework or as my prescribed oral topic.
- [ ] We have not already written on this topic in detail in class.

P

Appendix 3
French examples

Chapter 3, p18

La violence à la télévision

Sondage: répondez 'oui' ou 'non':

1. La télévision est une drogue.
2. Il y a trop de violence à la télévision.
3. On ne devrait jamais laisser les enfants seuls devant la télévision.
4. Les films violents rendent certains gens violents, les enfants aussi.
5. Les enfants ne savent pas la différence entre l'image et la réalité.
6. C'est la faute des parents si leurs enfants regardent trop la télévision.
7. Beaucoup de parents utilisent la télévision comme babysitter.
8. On devrait prévenir les téléspectateurs de la violence.
9. La violence à la télévision est quelquefois nécessaire et même utile.
10. On ne devrait pas censurer les films.

Chapter 3, p22

Some literary/cinematic vocabulary

un acte	act of a play
l'ambiance	atmosphere
l'auteur	author
le caractère	character (disposition)
la caractéristique	characteristic
le chapitre	chapter
le chef d'œuvre	masterpiece
la citation	quote
citer	to quote
la comédie	comedy

comique	comic
le comportement	behaviour
contemporain	contemporary
convaincant	convincing
le/la critique	critic
le décor	scenery
le dénouement	denouement
se dérouler	to take place
le dialogue	dialogue
le drame	drama/tension
le dramaturge	playwright
un écrivain	writer
émouvoir	to move
émouvant	moving
une époque	era
la farce	farce
la fiction	fiction
le genre	genre
le héros	hero
l'héroïne	heroine
l'histoire	story
l'humour (m)	humour
interpréter	to perform
l'ironie (f)	irony
jouer	to act
le lecteur	reader
la lecture	reading
le métaphore	metaphor
mettre en scène	to direct
la mise en scène	direction
le narrateur	narrator
l'œuvre	work of literature
se passer	to take place
le personnage	character (person)
le point culminant	climax
le portrait	portrait
le protagoniste	protagonist
réaliste	realistic
le récit	story
représenter	to depict
la représentation	depiction
le roman	novel
le romancier/la romancière	novelist
le siècle	century
(au dix-huitième siècle	in the eighteenth century)

la solution	outcome
le symbole	symbol
la technique narrative	narrative technique
la tendance	tendency
tendu	tense (adj.)

(*Source: Anneli McLachlan*)

Chapter 4, p31

Useful supplementary resources for research

Newspapers:
Libération
Le Monde

Magazines/other reading:
Phosphore
SAY Languages A level French topic packs
Que sais-je? Collection
Francoscopie
Le nouveau guide France
La France d'aujourd'hui

Educational magazines:
Authentik en français

Topic files:
SAY Languages A Level French topic packs

Videos:
Jeunes francophones (BBC)
Télétextes (OUP)
Le français par la publicité (Didier)
French express (C4)
Channel hopping (C4)

Appendix 4

German examples

Chapter 3, p22

Some literary/cinematic vocabulary

der Akt	act of a play
analysieren	to analyse
der/die Autor/in	author
der Charakter	character
das Drama	drama/tension
der/die Dramatiker/in	playwright
die Eigenschaft	characteristic
der/die Erzähler/in	narrator
die Erzählkunst	narrative technique
die Erzählung	story
die Figur	character
die Geschichte	story
das Gespräch	dialogue
die Hauptperson	protagonist
das Hauptthema	main theme
der/die Held/in	hero/heroine
der Höhepunkt	climax
der Humor	humour
der/die Ich-Erzähler/in	first person narrator
die Inszenierung	direction
die Ironie	irony
das Kapitel	chapter
komisch	comic
die Komödie	comedy
die Kritik	criticism
der/die Kritiker/in	critic
die Lektüre	reading
der/die Leser/in	reader

die Lösung	denouement
das Meisterwerk	masterpiece
die Metapher	metaphor
die Person	character
Regie führen	to direct
eine Rolle darstellen/spielen	to act
der Roman	novel
die Schilderung	portrayal
der/die Schriftsteller/in	novelist
die Spannung	tension
stattfinden (sep.)	to take place
(die Handlung findet in Wien statt)	(the action takes place in Vienna)
der Stil	style
das Symbol	symbol
die Szene	scene
das Thema	theme
vergleichen	to compare
das Werk	work of literature
zeitgenössisch	contemporary
das Zitat	quote
zitieren	to quote

(Source: Anneli McLachlan)

Chapter 3, p24

Ich bin der Meinung, dass ...	I am of the opinion that ...
Ich vertrete die Ansicht, dass ...	I am of the view that ...
Meiner Meinung nach ...	In my opinion ...
Was mich betrifft ...	As far as I'm concerned ...
Ich halte es für wichtig, dass ...	I consider it important that ...
Ich meine/glaube/finde/fühle, dass ...	I think/believe/find/feel that ...
Man muss in Betracht ziehen, dass ...	One must take into consideration the fact that ...
Tatsache ist, dass ...	The fact is that ...
Es ist immer der Fall, dass ...	It is always the case that ...
Obwohl diese Frage sehr umstritten ist, ...	Although this question is very controversial, ...

Chapter 3, p25

Das Fernsehen [11] ist eine gefährliche Droge zurück 1	Gewalt im [12] Fernsehen ist nötig in einer freien Gesellschaft	Die Werbung [13] hat keinen Sinn	Die [14] Pressefreiheit sollte nie beschränkt werden	Das Fernsehen [15] schadet der Vorstellungs- kraft
Die Geschichten [10] in den Boulevard- zeitungen sind zu aufgebauscht	Gewalt im [9] Fernsehen sollte strenger reguliert werden vorwärts 4	Seifenopern [8] verursachen eine starke Abhängigkeit	Die Presse [7] sollte strenger reguliert werden	Das Internet [6] verhindert die soziale Interaktion
Die Werbung [1] nutzt die Frauen aus	Man sollte [2] nicht glauben, was man in der Zeitung liest	[3] Das Fernshen gibt uns Denkanstöße	Die Werbung [4] gibt uns nützliche Informationen vorwärts 2	Die Presse [5] verteidigt unsere Rechte

Chapter 4, p31

Useful supplementary resources for research

Newspapers:
Die Zeit (weekly)
Süddeutsche Zeitung, especially *Jetzt* youth magazine

Magazines/other reading:
Brigitte
Juma
Der Spiegel
Stern
Inter Nationes resources
A level dossiers (available from the
Goethe Institut)

Books:
Deutschland nach der Wende

Educational magazines:
Authentik auf Deutsch
PZ
Wochenschau series

Videos:
Fünf Wochen im Herbst (about the reunification; available from the Goethe Institut)
Jung in Deutschland
TV Aktuell (OUP)
Turbo (C4)
The German collection: Advanced German (BBC)
Channel Hopping auf Deutsch (C4)
Turbo (C4)

Useful websites

Search engines:

(www.google.de) (www.lycos.de)

(www.yahoo.de) (www.abacho.de)

Newspapers:

(www.diewelt.de) (www.sueddeutsche.de)

(www.entry.de)

Search for and obtain a plethora of information about different regions, towns and cities in Germany.

(www.dw-world.de/german)

A fabulous site for accessing news and more general articles, including the chance to download audio and video files.

(www.tagesschau.de)

View the latest news bulletin, if you have a good enough Internet connection. Alternatively, listen to the news or visit the forum.

(www.goethe.de/z/jetzt)

Interesting texts and videos with exercises, maintained by the Goethe Institut.

Chapter 4, p35

NACHRICHTEN

1 Hören Sie den Nachrichten gut zu und füllen Sie die Tabelle aus!

Nachricht	Wer?	Wo?	Wann?	Was?	Wie?	Wie viele?	Warum?

2 Für jede Nachricht, schreiben Sie bitte die Schlüsselwörter.

Chapter 6, p51

WRITING CHECKLIST (German)

1. Have I checked nouns and do they have capital letters and the correct
   - genders?
   - plurals?

2. Do my adjectives agree?
   - have I got the right endings after *der/die/das/ein/mein*, etc and where there is no determining word?

3. Are my cases correct, especially:
   - direct (accusative) and indirect (dative) object pronouns?
   - have I added an -*n* to nouns in the dative plural?
   - accusative for motion, dative for place?

4. Have I used the correct prepositions?
   - governing the accusative, e.g. *für, durch*
   - governing the dative, e.g. *mit, zu*
   - governing either the accusative or the dative, e.g. *auf, an*

5. Have I checked my verbs?
   - do they agree with the subject?
   - do verbs in the past tense take *haben/sein*?
   - do regular verb forms follow the rules?
   - are irregular verb forms correct?
   - have I avoided mixing tenses?
   - have I used the correct tenses/tense sequence?

6. Have I checked my word order?
   - does the main verb come second in main clauses?
   - are past participles and infinitives at the end of the clause where required?
   - is the main verb in the final position in subordinate clauses?
   - have I obeyed the Time – Manner – Place rule?

Chapter 6, p52

Es spielt eine grosse Rolle, dass ...	It is significant that ...
Es ist kaum zu glauben, dass ...	One can hardly believe that ...
Es ist nicht zu leugnen, dass ...	One cannot deny that ...
Es ist immer/oft der Fall, dass ...	It is always/often the case that ...
Es kommt oft vor, dass ...	It often happens that ...
Es erhebt sich die Frage, ob ...	The question arises whether ...
Es kommt darauf an, ob ... ⎫	It depends whether ...
Es hängt davon ab, ob ... ⎭	
Einerseits ..., andererseits ...	On the one hand ..., on the other ...
Manche Leute sind der Meinung, dass ...	Some people think ...
Wie ich schon oben erwähnt habe, ...	As I have already mentioned earlier, ...
Es folgt daraus, dass ...	Consequently, ...

Chapter 6, p52

Über Statistik sprechen

die Zahl der ... stieg/erhöhte sich
the number of ... increased

die höchsten Steigerungsraten gegenüber dem Vorjahr wiesen ... auf
the highest increases on the previous year were in ...

jeder zwanzigste Deutsche gilt als ...
one in 20 Germans is considered to be ...

erstmals seit 1991...
for the first time since 1991 ...

die Zahl der ... beziffert sich auf ...
the number of ... amounts to ...

Source: Schauplatz © Brien, Brien, Christie & Schommartz (Heinemann Educational, 2000)

Appendix 5
Spanish examples

Chapter 3, p18

La violencia en la televisión

Encuesta: reacciona a las siguientes afirmaciones con un 'sí' o un 'no':

1. La televisión es una droga.
2. Hay demasiada violencia en la televisión.
3. Los padres nunca deben dejar a los niños solos delante de la televisión.
4. Las películas violentas causan violencia entre los mayores y entre los niños también.
5. Los jóvenes no aprecian la diferencia entre la imagen y la realidad.
6. Si los jóvenes ven demasiada televisión, la culpa está con los padres.
7. Muchos padres utilizan la televisión como canguro.
8. Deberían informar antes a los espectadores si hay episodios violentos.
9. En la televisión la violencia puede ser necesaria y aun útil.
10. No debemos cortar las películas para suprimir la violencia en ellas.

Chapter 3, p22

Some literary/cinematic vocabulary

el acto	act of a play
actuar	to act
el ambiente	atmosphere
el/la autor/a	author
el carácter	character (disposition)
la característica	characteristic
el capítulo	chapter
la citación	quote
citar	to quote
el clímax	climax
la comedia	comedy

cómico	comic
el comportamiento	behaviour
contemporáneo	contemporary
el crítico	critic
la crítica	criticism
el decorado	scenery
el desenlace	denouement
el diálogo	dialogue
dirigir	to direct
el drama	drama
el/la dramaturgo	playwright
el/la escritor/a	writer
conmover	to move
conmovedor	moving
la época	era
la farsa	farce
la ficción	fiction
el género	genre
la gracia	humour
el héroe	hero
la heroína	heroine
la historia	story
la ironía	irony
el lector	reader
la lectura	reading
la metáfora	metaphor
el narrador	narrator
la novela	novel
el/la novelista	novelist
la obra work	of literature
la obra maestra	masterpiece
un papel	role
desempeñar un papel	to play a role
el personaje	character (person)
pintar	to depict
el/la protagonista	protagonist
realista	realistic
el relato	story
retratar	to portray
el siglo	century
el símbolo	symbol
la trama	plot
la técnica narrativa	narrative technique
la tensión	tension
la tendencia	tendency

(*Source: Anneli McLachlan*)

Chapter 3, p24

En mi opinión …	In my view …
En cuanto a mí …	As far as I am concerned …
Creo/pienso/considero que …	I believe/think/find that …
Estoy convencido(a) de que …	I am convinced that …
No se puede negar que …	You cannot deny that …
Me parece que …	I think that …
Es poco probable que …	It is unlikely that …
No cabe duda de que …	There is no doubt that …
Para decir la verdad creo que …	To tell the truth I think that …

Chapter 3, p25

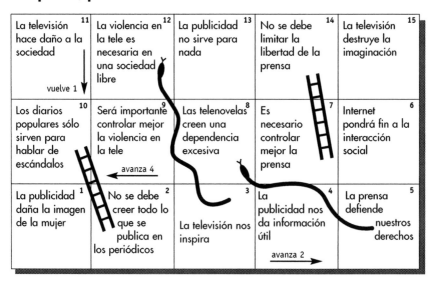

	11 La televisión hace daño a la sociedad vuelve 1	12 La violencia en la tele es necesaria en una sociedad libre	13 La publicidad no sirve para nada	14 No se debe limitar la libertad de la prensa	15 La televisión destruye la imaginación
	10 Los diarios populares sólo sirven para hablar de escándalos	9 Será importante controlar mejor la violencia en la tele avanza 4	8 Las telenovelas creen una dependencia excesiva	7 Es necesario controlar mejor la prensa	6 Internet pondrá fin a la interacción social
	1 La publicidad daña la imagen de la mujer	2 No se debe creer todo lo que se publica en los periódicos	3 La televisión nos inspira	4 La publicidad nos da información útil avanza 2	5 La prensa defiende nuestros derechos

Chapter 4, p31

Useful supplementary resources for research

Newspapers:
El País
El Mundo

Magazines/other reading
Cambio
Carta de España

A level topic study materials available from the education department of the Spanish embassy

Books:
El punto en cuestión, (Chancerel)
Aspectos del mundo hispano (Advance Materials)
España nuevo siglo (MGP)
Hispanoamérica ayer y hoy (SGEL)
España ayer y hoy (SGEL)
Spain 1812–1996, C J Ross (Arnold)
En el mundo hispánico (Chancerel)
Anuario El País book and CD-ROM
Serie FLASH, Acento editorial, monographs on subjects such as *las drogas, el cine español, la transición, el camino de Santiago, los jóvenes*

Educational magazines:
Authentik en español, newspaper, cassette and searchable Internet databank of articles

Video:
España campo y ciudad: Channel 4 video 2002, on Almería and Bilbao

Useful websites

Search engines/starting points:

www.msn.es

www.terra.es

www.rediris.es

http://es.yahoo.com

http://mx.yahoo.com

Language websites:

www.studyspanish.com

www.lenguaje.com

www.cvc.cervantes.es

www.el-castellano.com

www.diccionarios.com

Newspapers:

www.elpais.es   Madrid

www.elmundo.es   Madrid

www.lavanguardia.es   Barcelona

| www.elcomercio.com | Quito, Ecuador |

| www.lanacion.com.ar | Buenos Aires, Argentina |

Current news:

| www.rtve.es/tve/teletexto/index.html |

Spanish TV text, news and monographs

| http://news.bbc.co.uk/hi/Spanish/news |

BBC World in Spanish

Cinema:

| www.imdb.com |

| www.todocine.com |

Literature:

| www.rinconcastellano.es.org |

Chapter 4, p35

NOTICIAS

1 Mira/Escucha las noticias y rellena la tabla siguiente:

Noticia	¿Quién?	¿Dónde?	¿Cuándo?	¿Qué?	¿Cómo?	¿Cuántos/as?	¿Por qué?

2 Para cada reportaje, apunta las palabras clave.

Chapter 6, p51

WRITING CHECKLIST (Spanish)

1. Have I put accents where they are needed?

2. Have I checked the nouns, with regard to:
   - their gender, especially if ending in -*ma*?
   - the use of the article?
   - the right form of the plural?

3. Do my adjectives agree with the nouns, regarding both number and gender?

4. Do I have subject pronouns where necessary?

5. Are the object pronouns the right ones and in the right place?

6. Have I checked the use of prepositions?

7. Have I used the personal *a* where necessary?

8. Have I checked verbs, in particular:
   - radical changing verbs?
   - the correct use of the subjunctive?
   - do they agree with the subject?
   - are the strong preterites correct?
   - have I used a range of tenses?
   - is the sequence of tenses correct?

Chapter 6, p52

Dado que ...	Since/ because ...
Visto que ...	Since/ because ...
Puesto que ...	Since/ because ...
Ya que ...	Since/ because ...
Se puede que ...	It may be that ...
Aunque parezca curioso ...	Although it may seem strange ...
Por curioso que parezca ...	However strange it may seem ...
Esto demuestra que ...	This shows that ...
El resultado de todo esto es que ...	The result of all this is that ...
Queda claro que ...	It is obvious that ...
Esto nos lleva a concluir que ...	This leads us to conclude that ...

Chapter 6, p52

Hablar de la estadística

durante este periodo el número de ... ha aumentado/subido/disminuido/caído
in this period the number of ... has increased/risen/gone down/fallen

con respecto al año pasado, el aumento más significativo fue ...
with regard to last year the most important rise was in ...

el costo de la vida aumentó en un 5%
the cost of living rose by 5%

un 20% de los alumnos escolares sufren del estrés ocasionado por los exámenes
20% of pupils suffer from exam-related stress

un promedio/una media de 50 personas por día ...
an average of 50 people a day ...

uno de cada 10 colombianos ...
one in 10 Colombians ...

por primera vez desde el año 2001 ...
for the first time since 2001 ...